Owain Gwynedd
Prince of the Welsh

In memory of
Ifor Rowlands, Sir Glanmor Williams
and
Gareth Elwyn Jones

Owain Gwynedd
Prince of the Welsh

Roger Turvey

y Lolfa

First impression: 2013

© Copyright Roger Turvey and Y Lolfa Cyf., 2013

The contents of this book are subject to copyright, and may not be reproduced by any means, mechanical or electronic, without the prior, written consent of the publishers.

Published with the support of the
Thomas Edward Ellis Memorial Fund.

Cover image: Imaginary portrait of Owain Gwynedd
painted by Hugh Williams, 1909.
By permission of the National Library of Wales.

ISBN: 978 184771 694 1

Published and printed in Wales
on paper from well maintained forests by
Y Lolfa Cyf., Talybont, Ceredigion SY24 5HE
website www.ylolfa.com
e-mail ylolfa@ylolfa.com
tel 01970 832 304
fax 832 782

Acknowledgements

THE PUBLICATION OF THIS book was made possible by the generous financial assistance I received from the Thomas Edward Ellis Memorial Fund administered by the University of Wales.

I am grateful to Professor Prys Morgan and Professor Gareth Jones for their valued support and encouragement of my endeavours to bring Owain Gwynedd to print. My greatest debt is to Professor Ralph Griffiths on whom fell the unenviable task of reading and commenting on a draft of this book. His generous support and sound advice are very much appreciated. Needless to say, any remaining faults or flaws are entirely my own.

I wish to express my gratitude to the Very Rev. Dr Sue Jones, Dean of Bangor Cathedral, and especially to Mr David R. Price of Bangor. I am indebted to R.R. Davies, *Conquest, Coexistence and Change Wales 1063–1415* (Oxford, 1987) and W.L. Warren, *Henry II* (London, 1973) for the maps reproduced in this book.

I wish to thank Lefi Gruffudd and Y Lolfa for their willingness to take on this project and support its publication.

Finally, I wish to express my gratitude to my wife, Carol, for her wisdom, advice and unfailing support.

Contents

	List of Illustrations, Maps and Pedigrees	8
	Preface	9
I	The Gwynedd of Gruffudd ap Cynan	11
II	'Unconquered from his youth': Royal Apprenticeship	24
III	'Victories beyond number': War, Conquest and Expansion	34
IV	'Slayers of their enemies': Owain and Cadwaladr	51
V	A test of strength: Owain and Henry II	64
VI	'Faithful and devoted friends': Owain and Louis VII	84
VII	'Equity, prudence and princely moderation': Politics, Power and Princely Rule	96
VIII	'Making a good end': Death and Reputation	121
	Notes	135
	Bibliography	146
	Index	155

List of Illustrations, Maps and Pedigrees

Maps and Pedigrees:
1. Regional and Local Divisions of Medieval Wales
2. Gwynedd *c.*1105
3. Gwynedd *c.*1137
4. France and the Angevin Empire *c.*1160s
5. Gwynedd *c.*1170
6. The Dynasty of Gwynedd

Illustrations:
1. Artist's impression of Owain Gwynedd
2. Coat of arms of Owain Gwynedd in the choir stalls of Bangor Cathedral
3. Castell Tomen y Rhodwydd
4. Castell Cynfael
5. Llanrhystud Castle
6. Fourteenth-century manuscript depiction of Henry II and Thomas Becket
7. Memorial tablet to Owain Gwynedd in Bangor Cathedral
8. Plan of Bangor Cathedral by Gilbert Scott (1870)
9. The image of a Welsh king from *Cyfraith Hywel*
10. The images of Welsh kings from a fifteenth-century manuscript

Preface

THE GREATEST FIGURE OF the middle of the XIIth Century is certainly Owain Gwynedd; he and he alone, can form a central figure for the history of the time. From the death of Henry 1st in 1135 to the final overthrow of Welsh independence by Edward 1st, the three great national leaders are Owain Gwynedd, Rhys ap Gruffudd and Llywelyn Fawr.[1]

Thus did Owain Gwynedd's first 'biographer', Paul Barbier, estimate his subject's significance and eminence. Owain ap Gruffudd ap Cynan was certainly in good company though the omission of Llywelyn ap Gruffudd, commonly referred to as the Last, in this list of distinguished Welsh kings and princes might raise eyebrows today. Indeed, in the century since the publication, in 1908, of Barbier's *The Age of Owain Gwynedd*, it is Llywelyn who has found his historian and become the subject of an impressive biography.[2] Unfortunately, and ironically, Owain did not share in the good fortune that attended his father Gruffudd ap Cynan of Gwynedd, of whom a biography was written, a Welsh translation of a Latin original, some 30 years after his death. Approved, if not commissioned, by his son and successor Owain Gwynedd, the *Historia Gruffud vab Kenan* is the only near contemporary biography to be written for a Welsh ruler, or at least the only one to have survived. Loss, destruction, accident and sheer bad luck together with the good intentions of the unwitting and the unweary has conspired to reduce much of our written history to priceless fragments. Consequently, Owain Gwynedd has, undeservedly, slipped into obscurity partly because the evidence does not exist in sufficient quantity to support a biographical assessment of his life and career, and partly on account of the overwhelming interest in a later prince, Owain Glyndŵr. Nevertheless, from the evidence that does survive, it is possible to begin to reconstruct the lives and careers of great men such as Owain Gwynedd who played such a dominant role in the history of Wales before her conquest. Paul Barbier concluded his, otherwise sober and unromantic, study of Owain Gwynedd and the Wales in which he lived thus:

> There is a tendency to forget the great men of a conquered race. They are judged by the failure of their aims, once independence, that boon of peoples, is lost. They toiled indeed in the heat of the day; they seemed to live for their country's weal; they fought and died in its defence; but of what avail was it all, when the day of doom came, and that which they had laboured to preserve was lost forever.[3]

This short, popular study is intended as a modest first step towards ensuring that the deeds of a great Welshman are not forgotten.

The Gwynedd of Gruffudd ap Cynan

> And in that year [1072] Maredudd ab Owain was slain by the French and by Caradog ap Gruffudd ap Rhydderch on the banks of the river Rhymni.[1]

THUS DID THE NATIVE chroniclers announce the arrival of the Normans in Wales, not so much as conquerors but as allies in a domestic dispute between rival royal families. Wales was a politically and geographically fragmented country divided into rival kingdoms in which making war on one's neighbour was all too easy. On the eve of the Norman invasion of Wales, a long drawn out process that took more than two centuries to accomplish, the country was divided into several kingdoms — the most important being Gwynedd, Powys, Deheubarth and Morgannwg. The fluid nature of Welsh political life meant that some lesser kingdoms like Arwystli, Brycheiniog, Gwynllŵg and Rhwng Gwy a Hafren rose and fell subject either to absorption or conquest. However, just a few short years before the Norman triumph at Hastings in 1066, Wales had been united under the rule of a talented, powerful and charismatic, if ruthless, leader – Gruffudd ap Llywelyn. Indeed, if 1066 is an iconic date in English history witnessing as it did the death of Anglo-Saxon kingship and the establishment of Norman power, then 1063 is its equivalent in Wales. The death in that year of Gruffudd ap Llywelyn at the hands of Earl Harold Godwinson, who was himself killed by Duke William of Normandy three years later, brought an end to this unprecedented period of Welsh political unity. For eight years, between 1055 and 1063, Gruffudd ap Llywelyn had been, in the words of the Anglo-Saxon chronicle, 'king over all the Welsh'.[2] To the native chroniclers, Gruffudd, 'rex Britonum', had been 'the head and shield and defender of the Britons'.[3]

Whether he deserves to be considered, in the opinion of Frank Barlow, as 'one of the heroes of Welsh history' is debatable but there is no doubt that Gruffudd's death signalled the return of anarchy and dynastic war in Wales.[4] It was this competition for power following Gruffudd's death that led to Caradog ap Gruffudd ap Rhydderch's invitation to the 'French' to become his allies. Unfortunately for Caradog, his plea for assistance, in his struggle for control of the kingdom of Gwynllŵg, set in motion a process in which invitation was followed by intrusion and eventually invasion. Having set foot on Welsh territory, the Normans were loath to leave and it was not long before they began to act on their own initiative and fight with the object of obtaining title to large swathes of Welsh real estate. Thus Wales witnessed 'a great influx' of Norman adventurers, 'a crowd of busy pioneers, the flower of a people pre-eminently gifted as colonists, men not in the least afraid of the difficulties and dangers of Welsh campaigning'.[5] Sir John Edward Lloyd's eloquent description of the Normans is borne out by the evidence of their forceful campaigning in Wales. Described by a near contemporary Anglo-Norman chronicler, Orderic Vitalis, as 'innately warlike and bold', he goes on to say that the Normans 'would be invincible' if they were fortunate enough to be led and 'united under a good prince'.[6] These continental conquistadors certainly added a new and deadly dimension to the turbulent and bloody conflict that afflicted Welsh dynastic politics after 1063.

Caradog ap Gruffudd ap Rhydderch was but one among many ambitious men aspiring to rule more than simply a small and insignificant corner of their homeland. Among the most gifted, and persistent, of these noblemen determined to fill the void created by Gruffudd ap Llywelyn's death was Gruffudd ap Cynan of Gwynedd. Initially he was too young to participate in the scramble for power in Wales, being only eight years old in 1063, so he had to rely on the efforts of his family to keep alive his claim to the kingdom of Gwynedd. Much of what we know of Gruffudd's life and career comes from a near contemporary biography, the *Historia Gruffud vab Kenan*, the only one of its kind to have survived for a medieval Welsh ruler.[7] From it we learn that Gruffudd's mother, Ragnhildr, was the daughter of Olaf Sihtricson, king of the powerful Hiberno-Scandinavian community of Dublin. Gruffudd himself was born and brought up in relative safety in his mother's homeland of Ireland. His father, Cynan, had been forced to flee Wales after Gruffudd ap Llywelyn ousted, and perhaps killed, Iago ab Idwal ap Meurig in 1039 to take the kingship of Gwynedd. Less than a quarter of a century later Gruffudd ap Llywelyn would fall victim to an assassin's sword wielded it is thought by Iago's son Cynan.[8] As the son of Cynan and grandson of Iago, Gruffudd had a good claim to the throne of Gwynedd but his way was blocked by the two half brothers of Gruffudd ap Llywelyn, namely Bleddyn and Rhiwallon sons of Cynfyn. Although Bleddyn and Rhiwallon were, like their half brother Gruffudd, usurpers with no real claim to rule in Gwynedd other than by conquest, they were powerful enough to keep the nobility firmly in check.

Gruffudd had to bide his time and in 1075 the death of Bleddyn ap Cynfyn, following that of his brother Rhiwallon in 1070, gave him the opportunity to press his claim to Gwynedd. The succession of another outsider to the throne of Gwynedd, Trahaearn ap Caradog of Arwystli, may have proved a step too far for some of the nobility. It is possible that Gruffudd was encouraged to return to Gwynedd by the prospect of aristocratic support, which was forthcoming from the leading nobles of Anglesey and Llŷn. However, Gruffudd knew that this support alone would not be enough to dislodge Trahaearn and his ally Rhiwallon's son Cynwrig, so he followed Caradog ap Gruffudd ap Rhydderch's lead and forged an alliance with the Normans. By 1075 the Normans had settled in strength along the frontier between Wales and England and had begun to probe ever deeper into the Welsh heartland. The springboard for these infiltrations came via the three earldoms William I had established at Chester, Shrewsbury and Hereford. The earls and their knightly retainers were encouraged to make war on the Welsh and to annex their territory; in this way the natives could be contained and England protected.

The most powerful Norman lord in north Wales was Robert of Rhuddlan, a ferocious warrior who had carved out for himself a sizeable piece of Welsh territory stretching from the river Conwy to the banks of the Dee. With the aid of his equally fearless cousin Hugh of Avranches, earl of Chester, Robert had succeeded in establishing a town and castle at Rhuddlan on the site of a royal *llys* which became the *caput* of his rapidly expanding lordship. It is to Robert that Gruffudd turned for support which, ever the opportunist, the Norman readily offered. The alliance bore fruit in two victories, at Clynnog Fawr and Gwaederw, in which Cynwrig ap Rhiwallon was killed and a defeated Trahaearn was forced to flee Gwynedd and make for his native Arwystli. Establishing himself in Gwynedd, Gruffudd took the extraordinary decision to betray and turn on his Norman ally, Robert, whom he attacked at Rhuddlan. Unfortunately for Gruffudd, the leading men of Llŷn turned on him and, in alliance with the returning Trahaeran, they defeated him at the battle of Bron-yr-Erw. Seeking refuge in Anglesey, Gruffudd was pursued and eventually forced to flee back to Ireland.

Gruffudd returned from exile in 1081 and landed in Pembrokeshire. He was backed by a Hiberno-Scandinavian fleet and army, and supported by his ally, Rhys ap Tewdwr. Gruffudd and Rhys shared a common desire to regain their inheritance by occupying again the thrones of Gwynedd and Deheubarth respectively. They fought a pitched battle at Mynydd Carn in which their enemies, Trahaearn, Rhiwallon's other son Meylir and, bereft of his Norman allies, Caradog ap Gruffudd ap Rhydderch, were killed. After the battle Gruffudd made for Gwynedd but unlike his ally, Rhys ap Tewdwr, in Deheubarth, he failed to firmly establish his authority. Not only had Gruffudd to contend with his Norman adversaries but he had also to struggle with rival Welsh claimants such as Owain ab Edwin and his brother Uchtryd who hailed from Tegeingl.[9] Within months of his return he found himself a prisoner of the Normans. Gruffudd had been betrayed by one of his own men, Meirion Goch, and his captor may well have been Robert of Rhuddlan. Following his capture Gruffudd may have been among those Welshmen whom Robert 'kept for years in fetters' before being delivered into the hands of Earl Hugh who imprisoned him 'in the goal of Chester, the worst of prisons'.[10] He remained imprisoned for nigh on twelve years before escaping, sometime around 1093 or 1094 when he again laid claim to Gwynedd. In his absence Gwynedd had largely succumbed to the Normans who had extended their hegemony beyond the Conwy by establishing castles at Aberlleiniog on Anglesey and at Nefyn on Llŷn. According to the native chroniclers the Welsh

> being unable to bear the tyranny and injustice of the French, threw off the rule of the French, and they destroyed their castles in Gwynedd and inflicted slaughters upon them.[11]

A by-product of this general uprising of the Welsh against the Norman interlopers was the death in battle of Robert of Rhuddlan. It has been suggested, but cannot be conclusively proved, that Gruffudd may have been responsible for Robert's death.[12] Certainly, in the opinion of Orderic Vitalis, a hitherto unidentified 'Gruffudd king of the Welsh' led the raid that brought an end to the life of this 'swashbuckling Norman warrior'.[13] So serious had the situation become that King William II personally led two invasions of north Wales, in 1095 and 1097, both of which met with only limited

The Gwynedd of Gruffudd ap Cynan

success. Elsewhere in Wales, the floodgates had opened with the Normans pouring through to settle and plant castles in Ystrad Tywi, Ceredigion and Dyfed. This was due, in the main, to the death in 1093 of Gruffudd's erstwhile ally, Rhys ap Tewdwr of Deheubarth, who was killed resisting the invaders in the vicinity of Brecon.

In the ensuing chaos Gruffudd again attempted to secure his position in Gwynedd by military and marital means. Militarily, Gruffudd had gathered around him a small (perhaps no more than 160 men) but powerful force of household troops or *teulu*, upon whose loyalty he could count.[14] Never again would he be betrayed by one of his own. Additionally, he was able to raise an army or *llu*, recruiting men from as far afield as Llŷn, Eifionydd, Ardudwy, Rhos and Dyffryn Clwyd, all of whom, according to the *Historia*, 'received him as befitted their rightful lord' so that Gruffudd was now 'fortified with a large host around him'.[15] His marriage to Angharad, the daughter of Owain ab Edwin of Tegeingl was a significant step intended to draw the rivals into a mutual alliance. For a time, Gruffudd met with some success but three or four years of hard campaigning came to an end in 1098 when he was once more forced to seek sanctuary in Ireland. Fortunately for Gruffudd, this latest period in exile lasted less than a year, for in 1099 the Norman hold on Gwynedd was finally broken. While he was in Ireland gathering support, Gruffudd would doubtless have been delighted to hear that the man most responsible for ejecting him from his homeland, Hugh de Montgomery, earl of Shrewsbury, had been killed. The shock of Hugh's death, at the hands of marauding Scandinavian forces under the command of Magnus Bareleg, King of Norway, coupled with the rising tide of Welsh resistance, may have convinced his Norman ally and namesake, the earl of Chester, to withdraw from Anglesey and abandon the territory west of the river Conwy. Into this vacuum stepped Gruffudd ap Cynan who once more tried to stamp his authority on Gwynedd but only after 'making peace with the French' from whom he 'received Anglesey'.[16] Clearly, although the Normans had, temporarily at least, given up any immediate prospect of directly securing and settling Gwynedd, they had not abandoned the idea of exercising some form of overlordship of the region. That Gruffudd accepted this, preferring peace and a hazy, distant overlordship, suggests that he, like his Norman counterparts, may have been exhausted by the rigours of almost constant warfare.

Gruffudd needed time to consolidate his power if he was to secure his position as ruler of even a fraction of the kingdom of Gwynedd. His task was helped by the succession of Henry I to the English throne in 1100, the death in 1101 of his erstwhile foe, Hugh the Fat, earl of Chester, and, in the following year, the downfall of Robert of Montgomery, earl of Shrewsbury. The earldom of Chester entered a period of prolonged minority on account of the youth of Hugh's son and heir, while Henry I was determined to reach an accommodation, on his terms, with both the native rulers and Norman lords of Wales. Accordingly, so says the *Historia*, Henry I shortly after invested Gruffudd with the bulk of Gwynedd Uwch Conwy, namely, Llŷn, Eifionydd, Ardudwy and Arllechwedd.[17] This grant would have considerably enhanced his status and power, though it stopped short of cementing his rule in Gwynedd. The fact remains that Gruffudd was denied authority over the

The Gwynedd of Gruffudd ap Cynan

cantrefi that made up Gwynedd Is Conwy, namely Rhos, Rhufoniog, Dyffryn Clwyd and Tegeingl. This region, known also as the Perfeddwlad, part of which – Rhos and Rhufoniog – was once under the lordship of Robert of Rhuddlan, was retained by the earl of Chester who, with the Crown's active support, may have appointed Welshmen to rule there as his clients. Perhaps Owain ab Edwin and his sons were among them, since it is known they had retained some authority in Tegeingl and Dyffryn Clwyd.

Henry I was early in laying the foundation of his envisaged lordship of Wales in which there was to be a dualistic arrangement, whereby both Norman lords and native Welsh rulers were to recognise the authority of the English Crown. This did not stop Henry I continuing to exploit the rivalries of the Welsh rulers to keep them dependent. In Henry I the Welsh were to find a formidable opponent, a man who 'towers in the history of the subjugation of Wales and of the making of the Welsh March as no other monarch before the reign of Edward I'.[18] Henry was a master of manipulation who, according to Rees Davies, excelled at 'hoodwinking client princelings to act on the king's behalf while at the same time persuading them that they were acting in their own interests'.[19] Be that as it may, the fact remains that for the next 14 years Gruffudd was left in relative peace to make ever deeper the foundations of his power. The death in 1105 of his father-in-law, and potential rival for power, Owain ab Edwin, again helped to strengthen his position, though he did have to tread warily in dealing with his brothers-in-law, Goronwy, Rhiryd and Meilyr. In fact, it has been suggested that Gruffudd may not have been in sole charge of Gwynedd Uwch Conwy and that he was forced into some sort of power-sharing arrangement. This might explain why, in 1125, Gruffudd's eldest son, Cadwallon, 'slew his three uncles' so as to remove his rivals.[20]

If potential rivalry from within was difficult enough to manage, Gruffudd had also to keep a watchful eye on his Norman neighbours and anticipate the king of England's next move. That came in 1114 when, concerned at Gruffudd's growing strength, Henry mounted a major campaign against the Welshman and his then ally Goronwy ab Edwin. The pretext for invasion was provided by Hugh's son, Richard, newly come of age and eager to flex his muscles as earl of Chester. According to the Welsh chroniclers, Richard claimed, 'out of hate for them', that Gruffudd and Goronwy had raided and plundered his lands for which he expected some form of royal retribution.[21] Henry did not disappoint his vassal and an impressive show of military force was enough to bring both Gruffudd and Goronwy to heel. Both sued for peace and upon 'paying him [Henry I] a large tribute' the king was satisfied and they 'came to him and became his men and swore him loyal oaths'.[22] The Welsh were quickly coming to appreciate the fact that Henry I was a man not to be trifled with for as Orderic Vitalis reported:

> He inquired into everything and retained all he heard in his tenacious memory. He wished to know all the business of officials and dignitaries; and since he was an assiduous ruler, he kept an eye on all the happenings in England and Normandy.[23] [We might add, Wales too!]

Gruffudd remained loyal to his oath and did what he could to avoid provoking a king he knew to be more powerful and determined than himself. As other Welsh

The Gwynedd of Gruffudd ap Cynan

leaders fell foul of King Henry, Gruffudd remained aloof even to the point of refusing them shelter and protection when begged to do so. This attitude he applied even to one who had already, or soon would, become his son-in-law, namely, Gruffudd ap Rhys of Deheubarth. In 1115 Gruffudd and his brother Hywel fled to the perceived safety of Gruffudd ap Cynan's court, where according to the native chroniclers, 'Gruffudd received them kindly and gladly'.[24] However, on hearing this King Henry 'promised much good to Gruffudd ap Cynan for obtaining Gruffudd ap Rhys for him alive to be imprisoned; and if he could not get him alive to send him his head'.[25] The native chroniclers were outraged but not surprised 'as it was the custom of the French to deceive men with promises'.[26] Fortunately for the brothers, Gruffudd and Hywel, they were tipped off about Gruffudd's intentions and managed to evade capture. Six years of peace and growing prosperity were put at risk in 1121 when King Henry mounted a major campaign to punish the ruler of Powys, Maredudd ap Bleddyn. Maredudd and his nephews sought Gruffudd's aid but none was forthcoming for 'he, keeping peace with the king, said that, if they fled to the bounds of his territory, he would… oppose them'.[27] The threat of precipitate action had the desired effect and Gwynedd was left in peace.

> And after that Gruffudd governed for many years successfully and powerfully with moderation and peace, and enjoyed neighbourly relations in accord with the kings nearest to him, namely Henry king of England, Murchadh king of Ireland, and the king of the islands of Denmark.[28]

So stated the *Historia*, though it failed to mention that Gruffudd's policy of 'neighbourly relations' did not extend to his fellow Welsh rulers. By 1124 he had grown sufficiently strong as to test his military strength against those whose territories he coveted. Thus he embarked on a policy of territorial expansion and over the next 13 years the lordships or *cantrefi* of Meirionydd, Rhos, Rhufoniog and Dyffryn Clwyd played host to his war bands. These territories at least he could justly claim as having once been part of the ancient kingdom or kingship of Gwynedd but when the offensive turned south and east against Deheubarth and Powys, this was war for plunder and property, pure and simple. It was during this period that Gruffudd's sons make their appearance in the records. Cadwallon, Owain and Cadwaladr were young men, warriors all, with ambitions to follow their father as ruler of Gwynedd. During Gruffudd's lifetime there is a sense that co-operation, rather than discord, governed their relationship and that they had a shared aim of expanding the bounds of their kingdom. Indeed, it has even been suggested that the co-incidental appearance of Gruffudd's sons and the more aggressive policy towards Gwynedd's native neighbours was no accident: that it was they rather than the old king who were responsible for policy-making and for directing the kingdom's affairs after 1124. C.P. Lewis goes so far as to state that 'from the early 1120s until his death in 1137, he [Gruffudd] remained king in name but had handed effective authority to his sons'.[29] There may be some truth in this, but to suggest that his retirement can be dated to 1124 because 'he had given up leading his warbands in person' is perhaps wide of the mark and a little too early.[30] That he did relinquish his position at some point before his death is undeniable for, afflicted with blindness in his last years and, no doubt, physical difficulty given the age of 82 at which he died, Gruffudd would have wished to ensure a seamless transition of his power to his successor.

Gruffudd's achievements were many and the legacy he left for his successor was immense. He brought stability to the kingdom so that 'every kind of good increased in Gwynedd' enabling the people there 'to build churches… sow woods and plant them, cultivate orchards and gardens, and surround them with fences and ditches, construct walled buildings, and live on the fruits of the earth'.[31] The hyperbole of the author of the *Historia* notwithstanding, there is little doubt that Gruffudd's rule laid the foundations for Gwynedd's future strength, prosperity and expansion. He was certainly worthy of the praise heaped upon him by the native chroniclers who described him as the 'head and king and defender and pacifier of all Wales' who 'ended his temporal life in Christ… by making a good end in his perfect old age'.[32]

11

'Unconquered from his youth': Royal Apprenticeship

> By his [Gruffudd ap Cynan's] wife Angharad, the flaxen haired daughter of Owain ab Edwin, whom he married about 1095, he had three sons, Cadwallon, Owain and Cadwaladr, and five daughters, and about 1120 the two elder sons, it would seem, were old enough to take the field in place of their father.[1]

THUS DID SIR JOHN Edward Lloyd introduce Owain Gwynedd to the world in his classic study of the history of medieval Wales. There is little to alert the reader as to the impact Owain would have, not just on the history of Gwynedd, but on Wales as a whole. He was, in the opinion of J. Beverley Smith, 'a person of quite exceptional stature', the man who 'provided the foundations upon which later rulers of his dynasty used the supremacy of Gwynedd to secure a wider national unity'.[2] Yet for all his fame and achievements, and they were considerable, Owain is little known today outside his native north Wales, and even here his exploits have been overshadowed by those of his

'Unconquered from his youth': Royal Apprenticeship

princely descendants Llywelyn the Great and Llywelyn the Last. Indeed, in the minds of the twenty-first century Welsh public, the most famous prince of them all, and by far the best known, is Owain Glyndŵr. However, it is with another Owain that this study is concerned, a man whose historical rehabilitation is not only deserved but long overdue.

Unfortunately we know precious little about Owain's birth, upbringing and early life, and are therefore left with no choice but to speculate. The date of Owain's birth will forever defy precision but some suggestions may be made. If we accept J.E. Lloyd's date for the marriage of Owain's parents, then he is unlikely to have been born before 1095. Given the fact that he had an elder brother, and possibly, sister, we may settle for a date at or around the turn of the century. If this provides the earliest date for his birth, at the other end of the scale it is possible to suggest 1110 as a *terminus ad quem*. This latter date is based on the fact that the first mention of Owain by the chroniclers is in 1124 when he was engaged in a military expedition, which suggests that he was at least 14 years old.[3] This was the customary age for youths to be recruited, trained and blooded in battle.[4] However, if one considers the fact that Owain is mentioned alongside his elder brother Cadwallon, and that they were not only leading the expedition but commanding a *llu*, an army, rather than a *teulu* or war band, then it is possible to suggest that the younger of the two military leaders had some experience of war and was more likely to be in his late teens or even early twenties. If accepted, this would suggest a birth date for Owain of somewhere between 1100 and 1110. Either date would render redundant Paul Barbier's belief that at his accession in 1137 'Owain was now between

25

forty and fifty years old'.[5] Beyond this, speculation becomes a fruitless exercise, though it is worth noting that the author of Owain's entry in the *Dictionary of Welsh Biography*, Thomas Jones Pierce, favoured *c.*1100 as a likely birth date, whilst J.E. Lloyd's implication that Owain might have been active from about 1120 offers *c.*1106 as an alternative date.[6] As a final thought, the fact that Owain had fathered a son, Hywel, who by 1143 was considered old enough 'to fend for himself'[7] and be entrusted with military leadership and the rulership of a portion of Ceredigion, would favour Jones Pierce's suggested date of birth.

The place of his birth is equally shrouded in mystery, but again a few suggestions may be made. The Gwynedd in which Owain was born and brought up was war-torn and unstable, in short, a dangerous place in which to rear a family. In such circumstances it is likely that Owain's father, Gruffudd, would seek to ensure the safety and protection of his family by establishing his household in an area or region that was both loyal and, as far as conditions allowed, secure. The *cantrefi* with which Gruffudd is most usually associated are Môn (Anglesey), Arfon and Llŷn and of these, in the opinion of David Moore, 'Môn seems to have been loyal to Gruffudd most of the time'.[8] Indeed, he goes further, stating that, according to the chroniclers, even 'as late as 1121, Gruffudd is not mentioned as holding more than Môn'.[9] This is not to suggest that Gruffudd ap Cynan had not become master of virtually the whole of Gwynedd by the early 1120s, but rather it implies the central importance of Môn within his territorial authority. Given that Môn was the location of Aberffraw, the site of a royal *llys* with a long tradition, if not necessarily as long a history, as the principal

'Unconquered from his youth': Royal Apprenticeship

seat of the rulers of Gwynedd, it is not unreasonable to suggest that Owain might have been born here. Described by both chronicler and poet alike in words that carry an implicit invocation of historical antiquity, no more fitting a place than Aberffraw could surely be found to birth and rear a 'fine nestful of rulers'.[10] The significance of Aberffraw is captured in a poem by Meilyr Brydydd, Gruffudd's chief court-poet, who sang:

> At the court of Aberffraw for the fame of the fortunate one
> I sat on the couch beside the ruler.[11]

Very little may be said, or indeed, can be said, of Owain's upbringing but there is no reason to believe that it was anything but conventional. In common with others of his class, Owain would have received an education befitting a prominent member of the native aristocracy. This took cognisance of the fact that he was a warrior, a lord of men and a future ruler. This would have involved instruction in the principles of war, practice with the sword, the bow, lance and, of course, horsemanship. Owain would have feasted on a diet of war stories, war poems and war songs, and, as befitting an heroic society, he would have been imbued with the ethics of honourable war. Indeed, leadership in war was more than simply an expectation, it was one of the key determinants of royal status.

Alongside such an essentially military education, which was inculcated almost from birth, Owain and his brothers would have been taught the art of rulership. This involved more than just the power to command, since it included the ability to govern, to marshal resources, both financial and in kind, to make and enforce laws. Politics too would likely have found itself on the princely curriculum since the skills of diplomacy, negotiation and debate were becoming increasingly important tools in the hands of the more ambitious and capable rulers. It is possible that Owain received instruction in the liberal arts, the teaching of which was largely the preserve of the Church. That Wales had great men of learning is testified by the native chroniclers who lamented the death in 1099 of 'Rhygyfarch the Wise, son of Bishop Sulien, the most learned of the learned men of the Britons'.[12] Sixty-four years later, in 1163, the chroniclers noted the passing of Henri ab Arthen, 'an eminent teacher excelling all clerics'.[13] In fact, Wales had a tradition of scholarship that flourished in religious centres such as Llanbadarn Fawr and St David's, and although these schools were not as eminent or as celebrated as those on the continent, particularly Paris, they were, nonetheless, worthy of note.

Certainly, Owain's patronage of the Church, like that of his father, was generous, a fact that may reflect more than simply a pious regard for religion. Nor did Owain confine his generosity to the Church, the bards too were conspicuous recipients of his largesse and it may be significant that his father, Gruffudd, is linked by tradition to reforms in the practice of the arts of music and poetry.[14] Admittedly, this tradition can be traced back no further than the sixteenth century with the so-called 'Statute of Gruffudd ap Cynan', but that is hardly a compelling reason to dismiss entirely a link between Owain's father and the promotion of the liberal arts. Indeed, in the opinion of D. Simon Evans, Gruffudd's reign may be regarded as 'ushering in a new era in literature, religion, learning and politics', a part perhaps of what historians have

'Unconquered from his youth': Royal Apprenticeship

labelled the 'twelfth-century renaissance'.[15] Whether Owain was, like his contemporary Henry II, 'learned to a degree that was not only appropriate but also profitable to him', will never be known but it is worth noting the opinion attributed to another contemporary, Henry I, that an 'illiterate king is a crowned ass'.[16] This unflattering metaphor was repeated so often by contemporaries that, before the end of the century, it had become 'a cliché and a growing embarrassment to unlettered monarchs'.[17] If Owain was 'unlettered' it did not prevent him from appreciating the talents of those who were educated, particularly clerics well versed in Latin, the language of the Church, administration and of international diplomacy. These men were responsible for drawing up the few extant letters in Latin that Owain addressed to King Louis of France and Archbishop Thomas Becket of Canterbury. One of their number may also have been responsible for the Latin biography of Gruffudd ap Cynan, the *Historia Gruffud vab Kenan*, which is thought to have been composed during Owain's reign. At the very least Owain provided the kind of education in letters, literature and music that enabled his son, Hywel, to become proficient in poetic verse and thus join the esteemed ranks of the *gogynfeirdd*, the professional poets of their day.[18]

Perhaps the best teacher and the most stimulating environment in which to learn the arts of war, politics and government, was that provided by Owain's father, Gruffudd ap Cynan, at his court. Gruffudd's death at an advanced age in 1137, enabled Owain to spend nigh on 20 years in his father's company. This would have provided him with a valuable insight into the mechanics of rulership. Indeed, a close association with his father's court and government would have been a fundamental element in the instruction of the young prince, and intended as an apprenticeship for future rule. In fact, Owain was to learn early in his life what that 'apprenticeship' entailed, for it is clear that his marriage to Gwladus, the daughter of Llywarch ap Trahaearn, was no love match but a union arranged to cement the political partnership of Gwynedd and Arwystli. In the first quarter of the twelfth century Llywarch was a power to be reckoned with and a useful ally for Gruffudd ap Cynan as he sought to solidify his rule in an ever expanding Gwynedd. Although conjectural, Owain's marriage may have taken place sometime in or around 1124, for the native chroniclers state that Llywarch's lands were ravaged 'because he had helped the cause of the sons of Gruffudd ap Cynan and had made a pact with them'.[19] Owain's second marriage to Cristin, the daughter of Gronw ab Owain, may also have been politically motivated, designed to heal the bitter rift between the ruling families of Gwynedd and Tegeingl. Again, a date may be suggested for this second marriage, sometime after 1132, when Cristin's brother, Cadwgan, had settled his account with Owain's brother, Cadwallon, for the latter's slaying of his, and Cristin's, father, Gronw, in 1125. It was a lesson in political statecraft that Owain learned well for he, too, later embarked on a marriage policy designed to attract and attach, in close alliance, his fellow Welsh rulers.

It must be remembered that Owain was not alone in seeking the attention of his father and securing a place at court. His brothers, Cadwallon and Cadwaladr, were equally ambitious and they in all likelihood had their own interests to pursue. Nor can we rule out entirely the possibility that Owain, along with his brothers, might have spent a period

'Unconquered from his youth': Royal Apprenticeship

away from his father by being fostered out and reared in the household of a trusted nobleman. Fosterage has long been considered a key feature of medieval childrearing in medieval Wales, and more so in Ireland, and was a means by which the ruler could enforce the ties of fealty by binding the nobility into a closer and tighter relationship. Equally, in the opinion of Katherine Anderson, it was 'a way for nobles to prove their loyalty to their lord'.[20] Although the impact and influence of the institution of fosterage has been questioned by some historians[21] it must be pointed out that Gruffudd ap Cynan had himself been fostered, and there is evidence to suggest that Owain too followed this practice by fostering out his eldest son Hywel.[22] Even Gerald of Wales had something to say on the custom:

> [A] serious cause of dissension is the habit of the Welsh princes of entrusting the education of each of their sons to a different nobleman living in their territory. If the prince happens to die, each nobleman plots and plans to enforce the succession of his own foster-brother and to make sure that he is preferred to the other brothers.
>
> It follows that you will find that friendships are much warmer between foster-brothers than they are between true brothers.[23]

This can hardly be described as a ringing endorsement of the practice and his strictures are echoed in some versions of the native lawbooks, principally *Llyfr Cyfnerth*, where it is said that one of the *'teir pla cenedl'* [three plagues of kindred] is to foster the son of a lord.[24] If Gruffudd had seen fit to foster his sons it might help explain why the relationship between the siblings, especially that involving Owain and Cadwaladr, was so strained and often fractious.

It is not known which of his three sons Gruffudd ap Cynan intended to succeed him as king but if Owain nursed ambitions to follow his father as sole ruler of Gwynedd, he could not ignore the rival claims of his brothers Cadwallon and Cadwaladr. This meant that he must either eliminate or accommodate them. According to Welsh law the ruler had the right, almost certainly by the twelfth century, to appoint an heir-designate, known as *gwrthrych* or *edling*, who was, according to David Stephenson, 'to be the most privileged of the ruler's kin, the one who will rule after him'.[25] The fact that Gruffudd is described in the *Historia* as ruling his 'people with an iron rod, securing concord and peace' makes it unlikely that he would have risked his life's work by allowing others to decide the fate of his kingdom.[26] In the opinion of David Moore, 'That Gruffudd may have practised some form of designation is suggested by the fact that he was the first Welsh ruler to introduce appanage', a policy that was 'almost unique in twelfth-century Wales'.[27] Thus Gruffudd was prepared to apportion lands to each of his sons, a practice in keeping with the law of *Cyfran* or partible inheritance, but it seems the kingship was to remain inviolate and indivisible.

Unless one of his three sons showed exceptional ability leading to his selection ahead of the others, it is likely, though not certain, that the succession would be determined by primogeniture. As the eldest son, Cadwallon stood to inherit the kingship and it is instructive that when mentioned in the native chronicles he is invariably taking the lead; his brother Owain is clearly the junior partner in their expedition to Meirionydd in 1124, while Cadwallon alone is credited with slaying his uncles in 1125. The last we hear of Cadwallon,

'Unconquered from his youth': Royal Apprenticeship

in 1132, he is again striking out alone, campaigning in Nanheudwy, a lordship well within the bounds of Powys. This was to be Cadwallon's last expedition for he was killed by his cousins, Cadwgan ap Goronwy and Einion ab Owain, probably in revenge for the familial slayings of 1125. This left Owain as the next in line, if only on grounds of birth, and the fact that he appears to have enjoyed a relatively easy succession in 1137, at least to the satisfaction of most historians, may indicate careful planning either on the part of his father or by the heir himself. Death in battle may have removed Cadwallon from the succession but Cadwaladr remained a thorn in Owain's side. Not mentioned until 1136, he may have been much younger, and almost certainly less experienced than his siblings, which might account for his apparent acquiescence in Owain's assumption of power. Certainly the author of the *Historia* offers no hint of conflict between the brothers in their father's final days. As he lay dying Gruffudd

> blessed them and declared what kind of men they would be in the future. He commanded them to be brave and to resist fiercely their enemies, as he had done in his day.
> ... and then he died; and in Bangor was he buried in a tomb on the left side of the high altar in the church.[28]

III

'Victories beyond number': War, Conquest and Expansion

> Owain and Cadwaladr, leaders of Wales, led their host into Ceredigion, and they burned the castle of Walter de Bec and the castle of Aberystwyth... and they burned the castle of Richard de la Mare and the castle of Dineirth and Caerwedros. And thence they returned home happily jubilant.[1]

IN 1136 THE SONS of Gruffudd ap Cynan finally let loose their military on the unsuspecting alien communities of Ceredigion. Owain and Cadwaladr had for some time cast an envious eye on the fertile plains of this southern province but were deterred from acting on their warrior impulses by the knowledge that to do so would likely incur the wrath of the English king, Henry I. Two decades of relative peace and stability under Gruffudd ap Cynan had considerably strengthened Gwynedd and it was only a matter of time before that strength would be put to the test. By the 1130s the kingdom was ripe for expansion but in view of Gruffudd's advanced years and declining health, it

'Victories beyond number': War, Conquest and Expansion

was left to his sons to put into effect any policies in this direction. J. Beverley Smith's assertion that Owain 'had probably exercised a decisive influence in the kingdom of Gwynedd for some years before his accession' can readily be accepted, but Kari Maund is perhaps going too far in suggesting that 'he had been the architect of the expansion of Gwynedd in the 1120s and 1130s'.[2] This virtually ignores the contribution of both his brother, Cadwallon, and his father, Gruffudd, before death and, in the case of the latter, age and infirmity took their toll. Memorably described by J.E. Lloyd as a man 'as unscrupulous as he was energetic', Cadwallon may well have begun the process whereby the lordships of Rhos, Rhufoniog and Dyffryn Clwyd were annexed in the years after 1125 when he slew the region's three rulers, 'notwithstanding that they were his mother's brothers'.[3] That Henry I did not intervene suggests that he was either preoccupied or, more likely, was content to let the Welsh butcher each other. Indeed, it seems that as long as Anglo-Norman territories and their communities were left in peace, Henry turned a blind eye to native territorial ambitions so that the expansionist tendencies of Gwynedd were allowed to continue largely unchecked.

Given the state of their father's health it must have been obvious to both Owain and Cadwaladr that the issue of the succession would soon need to be resolved. Rivalry, jealousy and ambition are potent ingredients of dissension but, for the moment, and probably for as long as their frail father lived, the brothers set aside their differences and worked together to expand the bounds and enhance the authority of Gwynedd. These plans for expansion would be put on hold for as long as Henry I lived but with his death in December 1135, they were not long after put into effect. The first region to succumb to this more aggressive policy of expansion was, in all probability, Meirionydd. Although its annexation is not mentioned by the native annalists it is clear that at some point prior to 1136 – Kari Maund has suggested 1132 – this *cantref*, formerly a part of Gwynedd, had been secured by the northern dynasty.[4]

However, the bigger prize lay across the river Dyfi, where the agriculturally-rich lands of Ceredigion offered a tempting target and appeared ripe for either raid or conquest. Thus these 'two brave lions', these 'tamers of warriors' and 'paragons of strength' launched their devastating attack.[5] The praise lavished on Owain and Cadwaladr by the native scribes as they 'moved a mighty, fierce host into Ceredigion' in the spring of 1136, is due, in part, to the possibility that they were welcomed by the indigenous population as liberators rather than as conquerors.[6] The chronicle entries for this period may represent the work of a Llanbadarn-based scribe which, if this were so, would likely reflect the thoughts, hopes, and fears of the people of Ceredigion. In short, north Welshmen may have been marginally preferable to 'Norse Frenchmen'.[7] In the dismemberment of the kingdom of Deheubarth following the death of Rhys ap Tewdwr in 1093, Ceredigion had been claimed and conquered, though not securely settled, by Normans, Flemings and Saxons owing allegiance to the Clares, a family said 'to rank among the greatest of the Norman lords of the March'.[8] The first of the family to involve itself in Welsh affairs, Gilbert fitzRichard, lord of Clare and Tonbridge, did so by reason of the gift of Henry I, who offered him Ceredigion in 1110. If the Welsh had found a formidable opponent in Henry I, a man 'against

'Victories beyond number': War, Conquest and Expansion

whom no one could be of avail save God himself', then in Gilbert the Welsh were to meet an even more dangerous enemy, a man who had participated in one rebellion, in 1088, and conspired in another, in 1095, both against William II.[9]

When Henry I succeeded his brother as king of England in 1100, Gilbert, as tough as he was uncompromising, appears to have shown scant respect for the new monarch. In an extraordinary act of arrogance, Gilbert showed up at Henry's court where he 'bullied the king and his other courtiers'.[10] Within a few years Gilbert had been won over by the arch-manipulator, Henry, of whom it has been said that he 'seldom held a grudge when it was against his interest'.[11] Gilbert, 'brave, renowned and powerful, and a friend of the king', swept into Ceredigion and took all before him, building castles at the mouths of the rivers Teifi and Ystwyth.[12] His followers too soon erected their castles at strategic locations as the territory was divided up between them. Gilbert may not have lived 'very long to enjoy his new acquisition, but during the seven years of his rule he maintained a firm grip of Ceredigion'.[13]

However, following Gilbert's death in 1117, that grip was gradually to loosen, for though his heir, Richard, was no mean warrior himself, he lacked his father's gravitas and, significantly, his judgement. Richard fitzGilbert de Clare committed the unforgivable sin of arrogant complacency when he disregarded good advice to properly defend himself whilst travelling through potentially hostile Welsh territory. Gerald of Wales takes up the story:

> It happened a short time after the death of king Henry I, that Richard de Clare, a nobleman of high birth, and lord of Ceredigion, passed this way on his journey from England to Wales, accompanied by Brian de Wallingford, lord of this province [Abergavenny], and many men-at-arms. At the passage of Coed Grono and at the entrance of the wood, he dismissed him and his attendants, though much against their will, and proceeded on his journey unarmed; from too great a presumption of security, preceded only by a minstrel and a singer, one accompanying the other on a fiddle.[14]

Needless to say, the Welsh, no doubt incredulous at Richard's audacity, 'rushed upon him unawares' and killed not only him but many of his followers also.[15] It is ironic, if not perhaps fitting, that the man responsible for killing Richard de Clare, Morgan ab Owain of Gwynllŵg, was the grandson of Caradog ap Gruffudd ap Rhydderch, the Welshman who had first invited the Normans into south Wales in 1072.

News of the slaying of the Norman lord of Ceredigion, in April 1136, was the signal for Owain and Cadwaladr to lead their forces south over the river Dyfi. Among those participating in the raid were Hywel ap Maredudd of Brycheiniog, his sons, Rhys and Maredudd, and Madog ab Idnerth, lord of Maelienydd and Elfael. In a lightning campaign that witnessed the storming and burning of at least five castles, the brothers, 'happily jubilant', returned home. This was clearly a raid for plunder but also to test the defences, and the resolve, of the Norman knights who occupied the province.

If the Normans were found wanting in the first attack on their territory, they appeared no better prepared for the

'Victories beyond number': War, Conquest and Expansion

second which occurred at the end of the year. This time the sons of Gruffudd ap Cynan came not to raid but to conquer. If the native chroniclers are to be believed, the brothers had at their command a force consisting of 'about six thousand footsoldiers and two thousand mailed horsemen ready for battle'.[16] This was a formidable force that consisted of north Welshmen in alliance with the men drawn from across mid and south-west Wales, namely Brycheiniog, Maelienydd, Elfael and, significantly, Ceredigion and Ystrad Tywi. Success breeds confidence and feeds recruits which may explain why so many Welsh leaders were drawn to join Owain and Cadwaladr. The most prominent of those new recruits was Gruffudd ap Rhys ap Tewdwr, the dispossessed heir of Deheubarth and, by virtue of his marriage to Gwenllian, brother-in-law of Owain and Cadwaladr. Gruffudd had gone to Gwynedd to seek military aid in his war on the Normans but the price of that support may have been the ceding of Ceredigion, traditionally a part of Deheubarth, to the dynasty of Gwynedd. Unfortunately for Gruffudd, as he journeyed north his wife, Owain's sister, and two of his youngest sons perished in battle near Cydweli.

To secure Ceredigion, the Norman stronghold at Cardigan would have to be taken but its constable, Stephen, was determined to forestall a siege by meeting his opponents in a pitched battle. The fact that the Welsh obliged is indicative of their confidence and the progress made in their training, tactics and tenacity for, as one contemporary noted, 'the Welsh have gradually learnt from the... Normans how to manage their weapons and to use horses in battle'.[17] The battle at Crug Mawr, some two miles outside Cardigan, was a bloody affair which resulted in a complete victory for the

Welsh. When their ranks finally broke under the weight of the Welsh assault, the Anglo-Normans fled in terror towards the perceived safety of the town and castle of Cardigan, but many of them were caught and killed while others drowned in the river. According to Gerald of Wales, the Welsh vanquished their opponents because the latter were missing the leadership qualities of the recently murdered Richard fitzGilbert de Clare.[18] Of greater interest is Gerald's statement that the Welsh victory owed more to the generalship of Gruffudd ap Rhys than to the leadership of either Owain Gwynedd or his brother Cadwaladr.[19] Although Gerald's opinion cannot be disregarded entirely, it must be pointed out that as the bulk of the forces deployed at the battle were from Gwynedd, the accuracy of his assessment must be questioned.

The shock at losing this important battle cannot be underestimated, for the Normans, together with their Flemish allies lately settled in strength by Henry I in Pembrokeshire, had assembled a formidable force drawing volunteers, and doubtless conscripts, from across mid, south and west Wales, 'from the estuary of the Neath to the estuary of the Dyfi'.[20] Anglo-Norman scribes too took notice of the defeat of their countrymen but they, especially the anonymous author the *Gesta Stephani*, preferred to highlight Welsh atrocities perpetrated in the aftermath of the engagement

> with shouts and arrows they [the Welsh] pitifully slaughtered some, others they massacred by driving them violently into a river, a good number they put in houses and churches to which they set fire and burnt... old men they exposed to slaughter or mockery; the young of both sexes they delivered over to chains

'Victories beyond number': War, Conquest and Expansion

and captivity; women of any age they shamefully abandoned to public violation.[21]

It is not known if Cardigan Castle was taken, but the fact that the north Welshmen returned for a third campaign the following year suggests that it had withstood the earlier assault. Indeed, the expedition had cause to take and destroy a further three Norman castles in Ceredigion after which the men of Gwynedd pushed further south reaching as far as Carmarthen which was also captured and, presumably, destroyed. With the rich lands of the Tywi valley at their mercy, Owain and his brother spurned the opportunity to occupy, let alone hold it, they turned and headed north, content with the gains made in Ceredigion. It is possible that this was done as part of an arrangement which they had made with Gruffudd ap Rhys, and which, in spite of Gruffudd's death early in 1137, was likely continued with his eldest sons, Anarawd and Cadell. The third expedition to Ceredigion in 1137 came at a critical time, for it was launched in the months after the death of Gruffudd ap Cynan. Thus far the brothers had been operating, if nominally, in the name of their father, the king, but henceforth Gruffudd's successor would shape and direct Venedotian policy.

The alliance with their nephews, Anarawd and Cadell, was renewed in the next expedition to Ceredigion in 1138 when Owain and Cadwaladr tried once more to take Cardigan Castle. They besieged the fortress by land and by sea, enlisting the aid of a Hiberno-Scandinavian fleet of 15 ships in the process, but to no avail: Cardigan held out.[22] In spite of this reverse, the brothers managed to complete the conquest of Ceredigion, taking or

41

destroying all the castles in the province while isolating Cardigan. The annexation of the province was followed by its division between Owain's eldest son Hywel, who received all the land south of the river Aeron, and Cadwaladr, who received the territory between the Aeron and Dyfi. Cadwaladr's share of the spoils was significantly larger than that allotted to Hywel, which may reflect his status within the royal family or *membra Regis* as the king's brother. Equally it might be indicative of Cadwaladr's strength that Owain dare not snub his brother for fear of provoking him into taking some precipitate action. On the other hand, it might have been an attempt by Owain to deflect his brother's attention and energies away from Gwynedd. Whatever the reason, it suggests that Owain was conscious of the fact that his brother might be nursing more than simply a grudge or grievance but also a burning desire to supplant him. Cadwaladr had an important part to play in the matrix of power in Gwynedd; he could not be silenced and nor could he be ignored.

If there was growing tension between Owain and Cadwaladr it was not immediately apparent, in contrast to England where the death of Henry I had precipitated a crisis in which the succession was disputed between two rival claimants. The dispute between Henry's daughter and heir, Matilda, and her cousin, Stephen of Blois, escalated after the latter was crowned king of England. Civil war broke out and the kingdom descended into chaos if not, at times, an oft-quoted anarchy.[23] It is to the period between the death of Henry I, on 1 December 1135, and the murder of Richard fitzGilbert de Clare, on 15 April 1136, that the Welsh chroniclers appear to date the collapse of English power in Wales. The West Country based-author of the

'Victories beyond number': War, Conquest and Expansion

Gesta Stephani is even more precise, citing the annihilation of an Anglo-Norman army near Loughor on 1 January 1136 as the beginning of what it called the great uprising of the Welsh.[24] Distracted by rebellion at home and conflict abroad, most notably in Normandy, Stephen had neither the time nor the resources to deal with the Welsh. Stephen's only response to the deteriorating situation in Wales was to dispatch Baldwin fitzGilbert de Clare, Richard fitzHarold of Ewyas, and Earl Robert of Gloucester, with orders to re-fortify and re-supply the garrisons of south and west Wales, including Cardigan Castle.

As the younger brother of the recently murdered Richard, Baldwin de Clare was granted Ceredigion by the king in the hope that this would induce him to fight for it. Supported by a large mercenary army, Baldwin got no further than Brecon before reporting to King Stephen that Wales, let alone Ceredigion, was lost. Nor was he exaggerating for according to the English chronicler, John of Hexham, during the autumn of 1136 'the Welsh, laying waste the border areas of England killed two barons' after which they made peace with King Stephen.[25] The Crown's response to this killing convinced the Anglo-Norman Marcher Lords that they were on their own. It was during this time, the late autumn of 1136, that the Anglo-Normans scored a solitary success when Miles of Gloucester, from his base at Brecon Castle, dashed across country to relieve the garrison at Cardigan Castle and rescue Adeliza, the widow of Richard fitzGilbert de Clare. In an ironic twist, this same Adeliza is thought to have later married Owain Gwynedd's brother, Cadwaladr. Unlike his predecessor Henry I, Stephen was neither as dominant nor as commanding, nor could he make and break individuals and families. Further trouble was heaped on the shoulders of the hapless king when Payn fitzJohn, sheriff of Shropshire and one of Henry I's most trusted lieutenants in the Welsh March, was killed in July 1137 when attempting to recover Carmarthen for the Crown. It was around this time, according to John of Hexham, that Ranulf, earl of Chester, is reported to have narrowly escaped capture by a Welsh raiding party.[26]

Gwynedd stood to benefit most by King Stephen's discomfiture because it had had the time to consolidate and grow strong in the previous two decades. Owain Gwynedd was quick to seize the initiative and take advantage of the distractions and problems confronting the English king. The landing in Sussex of Stephen's nemesis, the Empress Matilda, and her army, on 30 September 1139, would likely have encouraged Owain to be bolder still in his territorial ambitions. Having all but secured Ceredigion, Owain turned his attention to the north-east where the prospect of securing the lordship of Tegeingl and commote of Ystrad Alun beckoned. The territories were all that was left to the earls of Chester after the initial inroads into north Wales during the last quarter of the eleventh century had been overturned by the resurgence of Welsh power under Gruffudd ap Cynan. Having only recently routed a formidable Anglo-Norman army near Cardigan, the enemy, 'warlike and bold' though they may be, were no longer as 'invincible' as they once were perceived. Owain did not charge headlong into a military confrontation, nor did he raid the region; rather he adopted a more subtle approach in his politicking. In surveying the political landscape it is possible that he concluded that Earl Ranulf of Chester

'Victories beyond number': War, Conquest and Expansion

would likely be drawn into the civil strife that had begun in earnest with Matilda's entry into the kingdom. In a remarkable turnaround in fortunes, it was the Welsh who now offered themselves as allies of their Anglo-Norman neighbours and who became embroiled in a domestic dispute between dynastic rivals in England. Orderic Vitalis notes, disapprovingly, the way in which those who were opposed to King Stephen made allies of whomsoever was prepared to support them:

> The most powerful of the rebels recklessly steeled themselves to resist, and entered into an alliance with the Scots and Welsh and other rebels and traitors, bringing down ruin upon the people.[27]

Owain's offer of military support was gratefully accepted, but it was his brother Cadwaladr who led the contingent of north Welshmen east towards the fighting in Lincolnshire. It has been suggested, most notably by J.E. Lloyd, that Cadwaladr's involvement in the English civil war was his decision alone and that 'it may be doubted whether Owain approved of the adventure' because the whole enterprise was 'all to the profit of the great border lords, followers of the Empress Matilda'.[28] This view is rather short-sighted for, in truth, Owain had much to gain by involving himself in the civil strife in England. A distracted king and Marcher nobility, including the earl of Chester, would suit Owain; the longer the war lasted, the better for him. By dispatching Cadwaladr to England, Owain was not only ridding himself, at least temporarily, of a problem, but was encouraging his brother to expend his considerable energies in battlefields far from the borders of Gwynedd. Indeed, it might have occurred to him that his younger sibling might meet his end in battle and be buried in a far-flung corner of a foreign field. Although a touch Machiavellian in its design, it might also be suggested that Owain was calculating his options should either side win the battle, if not the war. If Stephen were to be victorious, then Owain could claim that no blame should attach itself to him since Cadwaladr acted alone but, if the reverse should happen, then the Empress Matilda would be in his debt.

It may be doubted that such a significant military intervention could have been taken without the approval or sanction of Owain who, after all, would likely have been asked to furnish troops additional to those commanded by Cadwaladr. The latter would undoubtedly have taken his *teulu* or household troops, but as these would perhaps have numbered between 50 and 300 men, a more substantial force would have been necessary to stir the interest of Earl Ranulf and his allies.[29] Cadwaladr was joined by other native contingents led by Morgan ab Owain of Gwynllŵg and, if the identification is correct, Madog ap Maredudd of Powys.[30] In the opinion of John of Hexham the combined Welsh force was substantial enough to make up to a half of the army assembled against King Stephen.[31] Battle was joined on 2 February 1141 outside the city of Lincoln and, assisted by a contingent of what the author of the *Gesta Stephani* described as the 'untamed savagery of the Welsh', Earl Ranulf's forces were triumphant.[32] King Stephen's forces were routed, he was captured and the city was sacked. The Welsh had certainly made an impression on the local inhabitants of the city and its environs for, as Orderic Vitalis relates:

'Victories beyond number': War, Conquest and Expansion

> More than 10,000 *barbari* (as they are called) were let loose over England and they spared neither hallowed places nor men of religion but gave themselves up to pillage and burning and massacre. I cannot relate in detail what sufferings the church of God endured in her sons, who were daily slaughtered like cattle by the swords of the Welsh.[33]

It is a bittersweet irony that one of those nobles captured by the Welsh, alongside Stephen, was Baldwin fitzGilbert de Clare, the man who had failed to relieve Cardigan Castle let alone rescue his sister-in-law some five years earlier but who, prior to the battle, had urged his men not to fear the Welsh. Given the folly and subsequent murder of his brother Richard, distain for the Welsh clearly ran deep in this family!

Perhaps the one eventuality that Owain had overlooked was that Cadwaladr might return in triumph and thereby attract admirers and supporters. This made his brother more dangerous rather than less, especially as he had begun to cultivate the likes of Earl Ranulf and others of the English nobility as friends and allies. Certainly he seemed invigorated by his English adventure and perhaps thought that he could push the limits of his power by acting contrary to his brother's wishes. Cadwaladr's murder of Anarawd in 1143 put at risk the alliance which Owain had forged and maintained with the sons of Gruffudd ap Rhys of Deheubarth. No reasons are given by the chroniclers to explain Cadwaladr's action, but it led to a rupture in relations with his brother who turned on him. As if mirroring the events in England, Gwynedd too descended into civil war which, although short-lived – it was over before the end of 1144 – must have checked Owain's ambitions in the north-east. Fortunately for Owain, the alliance with the young dynasts of Deheubarth held firm, and he dispatched his son Hywel with an army south to assist his patient and understanding allies. There, in 1145, Hywel distinguished himself by winning a 'fierce battle' near Cardigan after which he and his brother Cynan 'returned bearing with them great spoil'.[34] A year later Hywel returned south where he campaigned successfully until the middle or end of 1147, before returning north to confront his uncle Cadwaladr in a further outbreak of civil strife.

With his son campaigning in south Wales, Owain had been busy putting into effect his long-held plans for the seizure of Tegeingl which he is thought to have accomplished sometime in 1146. Certainly, by the end of August of that year, his erstwhile ally, Ranulf, earl of Chester, was concerned enough by the scale of the Welsh attacks to request help from the man he had humbled at, and imprisoned after, the battle of Lincoln five years earlier, King Stephen. Released from his captivity in November 1141, Stephen had endured imprisonment for nigh on nine months, during part of which he had been shackled, so he was understandably wary of Earl Ranulf. A deeply suspicious Stephen not only refused Ranulf's request for help against the Welsh, but seized and imprisoned him at Northampton. The Welsh seemed to be carrying all before them in Tegeingl and it is perhaps no coincidence that as news of Ranulf's detention spread, Owain seized the initiative and stormed the earl's castle at Mold in the neighbouring commote of Ystrad Alun.

Having dispatched the Anglo-Normans and restored the ancient boundary of Gwynedd along the river Dee, almost up to Chester itself, Owain now turned his attention to

'Victories beyond number': War, Conquest and Expansion

his neighbour Madog ap Maredudd of Powys. Control of Ystrad Alun and Dyffryn Clwyd enabled Owain to launch an attack, in 1149, on the lordship of Iâl which was quickly overrun and in which he built a castle. The sheer size of the castle at Tomen y Rhodwydd suggests that this was no mere raid but an attempt by the men of Gwynedd to annex the lordship. In short, they were there to stay. Aware of the seriousness of the situation, Madog sought the help of the now released Earl Ranulf and between them they hoped to dislodge Owain from both Iâl and Ystrad Alun, perhaps even from Tegeingl. At the battle of Coleshill in 1151 Owain crushed the Cambro-Norman army, many of which had been slain whilst 'the others turned their backs in flight'.[35]

By the beginning of 1152 Owain had succeeded in restoring Gwynedd to her pre-Norman boundaries whilst adding territories seized from Powys and Deheubarth. It was a significant achievement but its longevity was put in jeopardy by the death of Stephen and the accession of the Angevin, King Henry II. Henry was everything Stephen was not – strong, decisive and blessed with a charisma that commanded respect and obeisance. Henry was determined to turn the clock back and restore the Crown's power and authority in Wales to a position it had enjoyed prior to Stephen's reign. Something of the mindset and attitude of the men employed to accomplish this task is captured in a contemporary account:

> You shall have my lands in Wales, which is a land of strife and warfare. By your courtliness you will civilize the ill-nature of the natives.[36]

However, as events were to show, Henry II had underestimated his uncivilised and ill-natured foe, and his campaigns in Wales, four in total between 1157 and 1165, did not meet with unqualified success. According to one Anglo-Norman chronicler, the reason why the Welsh proved so difficult to master and reduce to obedience was that success in war had bred in them a confidence that bordered on arrogance. They no longer feared the 'French' and had become 'the stern masters of those before whom a little earlier they had bent compliant necks'.[37] The scene was set for a titanic struggle.

IV

'Slayers of their enemies': Owain and Cadwaladr

> Owain and Cadwaladr, sons of Gruffudd ap Cynan...
> were the splendour of all the Britons... the men who were
> two exalted kings and two generous ones, two fearless ones,
> two brave ones, two fortunate ones, two pleasant ones, two
> wise ones, protectors of the churches and their champions...
> and who were jointly upholding together the whole
> kingdom of the Britons.[1]

IT IS ABUNDANTLY CLEAR that in the mind of the native scribe responsible for penning this description of the sons of Gruffudd in 1136, Owain and Cadwaladr were equals, 'two exalted kings', and partners 'jointly upholding' the cause of Gwynedd. This impression of joint kingship is supported by the Anglo-Norman writer, Orderic Vitalis, a contemporary of Owain and Cadwaladr who he described in 1141 as kings of Gwynedd.[2] This would suggest that the kingship as well as the kingdom had been divided between them. Certainly the doyen of Welsh medieval historians, Sir J.E. Lloyd, believed that some kind of partition had taken place after the death of Gruffudd ap Cynan:

> Welsh sentiment forbade him [Gruffudd] to bestow the whole of his kingdom upon his eldest son, Owain, and thus a division with Cadwaladr took place which sacrificed the unity of Gwynedd and gave rise in course of time to serious disputes.[3]

Lloyd confined his comments to the partition of the kingdom, that is, the landed inheritance, rather than the division of the kingly office, the kingship. Given the Welsh custom of partible inheritance or *cyfran,* by which landholdings were divided up equally between siblings after the death of the landholder, Lloyd can be forgiven his silence on the fate of the kingship. Not so Goronwy Edwards, who stated that 'the succession to the kingly or princely office in Wales was not determined by any adequately defined rules' and that although 'it was in a general sense hereditary… there was no fixed rule of primogeniture'.[4] As far as Goronwy Edwards was concerned, Welsh law only allowed for one interpretation namely, 'that the lands of a king or prince were at his death divided… among all his male heirs' with the result that 'the maximum opportunity was given for the interplay of personal ambitions and rivalries among the heirs of the princes'.[5] The interpretations applied by both Lloyd and Edwards to the texts of the Welsh laws are no longer regarded as unimpeachable though they still have their champions among some modern historians. For example, David Crouch is firmly of the opinion that in Wales the 'kingship was divisible between siblings, as Owain and Cadwaladr ap Gruffudd ap Cynan demonstrated after 1137'.[6] However, the idea of a divisible kingdom let alone a divisible kingship does not find favour with the majority of historians. According to J. Beverley Smith, 'Cadwaladr had no share in the *regnum*' and goes on to explain that those sections of the

'Slayers of their enemies': Owain and Cadwaladr

Welsh lawbooks that deal with partible inheritance were not so much concerned 'with succession to kingdoms but with the practice which applied to the lands of free proprietors'.[7] As far as the kingship is concerned, he believes that:

> Historians have burdened us with the view that Wales was a land where there were unalterable rules which provided that the royal estate was subject to partible succession, that there were laws which ordained that kingdoms and principalities should be sundered by partition. However, the lawbooks strongly imply that the *regnum* or kingship was indivisible.[8]

Indeed, one might argue that when the author of the *Brut y Tywysogyon* penned his tribute to the joint leadership of Owain and Cadwaladr in 1136, Gruffudd ap Cynan was ailing but very much alive, so in that respect the brothers might well be described as equals. No hint here of Owain's seniority to, or, as events transpired superiority over, Cadwaladr; for the moment, and probably for as long as their aging father lived, they set aside their differences and worked together for the good of Gwynedd. Although Orderic Vitalis wrote four years after the death of Gruffudd ap Cynan, his description of the sons as joint kings is tempered by the fact that he was writing as an outsider and his impression may have been coloured by rumour, informed by misinformation and shaped by a degree of ignorance.

Disputed succession and territorial fragmentation were facts of Welsh political life during the twelfth and thirteenth centuries but the accepted wisdom is that the kingship remained intact and passed to Owain who, as the best-positioned heir, succeeded his father as king of Gwynedd. Doubtless Cadwaladr was less than pleased with the prospect of his elder brother's succession but by a combination of luck and political acumen, Owain was able to outwit and, later, when they came to blows, defeat his brother, along with other potential rivals, to become sole ruler of Gwynedd. Needless to say, their relationship after 1137 was a troubled one but, initially at least, Cadwaladr had to be content with a lesser, if not insignificant, role. If the kingship remained indivisible and beyond Cadwaladr's grasp, a share of the kingdom was not. As befitting a senior member of the royal family or *membra Regis,* Cadwaladr was entitled to a portion of the patrimonial inheritance and, on Owain's succession, he was granted, or confirmed in possession of Anglesey and Meirionydd, and quite possibly the commote of Dinllaen in Llŷn.[9] This did not amount to a partition of the kingdom since these lordships, or *cantrefi,* were held by Cadwaladr of his brother, the king. In essence Cadwaladr had been granted an apanage within the borders of the kingdom to which was added the northern part of Ceredigion a year later, in 1138. Territorially Cadwaladr had been well provided for which Owain doubtless hoped might satisfy his brother: he was wrong. In truth, and in spite of his brother's generosity, the territorial inheritance fell far short of Cadwaladr's ambition: the kingship of Gwynedd.

Hindsight, allied to human nature, might persuade us that Owain and Cadwaladr were naturally antagonistic and rivals even before their father's death in 1137, but the evidence, such as it is, does not admit to any serious difficulty until 1143. In that year Anarawd ap Gruffudd, the eldest son of Owain's late brother-in-law, Gruffudd ap Rhys, was killed by members of Cadwaladr's *teulu.* It is not known if the murder of Anarawd was ordered by Cadwaladr and, if so,

'Slayers of their enemies': Owain and Cadwaladr

why, but the fact that it was committed by his 'followers' or 'war band' meant that he was held responsible.[10] The incident had the potential to seriously harm, if not break, the hitherto close relations between Deheubarth and Gwynedd. Owain had striven hard to forge a military and political alliance with the young dynasts of Deheubarth, to the extent that he was in the process of arranging a marriage between his daughter and Anarawd. According to the native chroniclers, Owain, on hearing of the murder, 'took it grievously' and he resolved to dispossess Cadwaladr of his territory.[11] As Owain took possession of Anglesey, his son, Hywel, doubtless acting on his instructions, attacked and burned Cadwaladr's castle at Aberystwyth and seized his portion of Ceredigion. Cadwaladr was forced to flee the kingdom and, like his father before him, he sought shelter in Ireland.

On reaching Dublin in 1144, he made contact with the sons of the powerful Hiberno-Scandinavian chiefs, Otir, Turcaill and Cherwulf, and persuaded them to aid him in his quest for the restitution of his lands in Gwynedd. It is possible that at least one (if not all) of these men was already known to Cadwaladr, who may have employed them in the siege of Cardigan six years before. A substantial troop of mercenaries was assembled, supported by a naval task force, both of which subsequently made their way to Abermenai in Gwynedd. The choice of Abermenai as an embarkation point is intriguing since it was one of the properties bequeathed by a dying Gruffudd ap Cynan to his wife Angharad. Clearly it was thought a safe place to land, which might suggest that Cadwaladr's enterprise had the support of his mother. Certainly someone was responsible for healing the rift between the brothers before a blow had been struck in anger. According to the native chroniclers, 'Owain and Cadwaladr made peace through the counsel of their leading men, as befitted brothers' which was likely true, but one should not perhaps discount entirely the influence or intervention of their mother, the queen dowager.[12] Civil war was avoided and Cadwaladr's lands were restored to him, but it was clear that in accommodating his brother, Owain was not yet in a position to exert uncontested power over Gwynedd.

Having settled their differences, the brothers had to face the wrath of the mercenary troops hired by Cadwaladr in Dublin. To be denied the victory and booty they had expected was simply too much for the Irishmen to bear. They were not prepared to go home quietly without something tangible to show for their efforts, and when Cadwaladr attempted to negotiate a peaceful withdrawl, he was seized and held to ransom. The price of freedom was high: his erstwhile allies demanded delivery of 2,000 cattle with captives and perhaps a sum of money to sweeten the deal. Cadwaladr duly obliged and he was released and upon receiving the news his brother Owain fell

> upon the Irishmen, and slewe a great number of them, and recovered all the cattell with the prisoners and other spoyle, and as many as escaped alyve returned home with great shame and losse.[13]

This action probably put paid to any future alliance between the dynasts of Gwynedd and those of Dublin. In some respects this had reduced the options available to Cadwaladr should he and his brother fall out again. There

'Slayers of their enemies': Owain and Cadwaladr

is no reason to doubt the fact that relations between the brothers were strained but, for three years at least, peace reigned between them.

That peace was shattered in 1147 when Hywel and Cynan launched an attack upon their uncle and took Meirionydd from him. Contemporaries are largely silent on the motive behind this assault, other than to say that 'there was strife' between the sons of Owain and Cadwaladr.[14] The chroniclers are more concerned to relate the fate of Cadwaladr's castle at Cynfael which was closely besieged. The castle constable was one Morfran, the head of the *clas* church at nearby Tywyn, who, in spite of his religious vocation, was a man as skilled in the arts of war as he was in the ways of prayer. The besiegers tried to induce Morfran to surrender, initially by using bribery, offering him 'many gifts', and when this failed by 'harsh threats'; he would have none of it preferring 'to die honourably than to lead a life of shame through treachery to his lord'.[15] The castle was eventually taken after a vicious fight in which many were killed and wounded, though Morfran managed to escape in the confusion. Was this a personal quarrel or had Hywel and Cynan acted on instructions issued by their father? There is no clear answer to this question, but there is every reason to suspect that Owain was complicit in the attack if not its prime mover. To suggest otherwise is to admit to a serious breakdown in Owain's authority to a point where he had lost control of his sons. Although this is not impossible, at least temporarily, Owain's subsequent career points to its improbability. That said, the period between 1147 and 1152 witnessed a rising tension within the royal family that spilled over into violence.

Having dispossessed Cadwaladr of Meirionydd, it is not known if the lordship was ever restored to him, three years later, in 1150, Hywel seized his uncle's former lands in Ceredigion. The pretext for this act of aggression is not known but it might have something to do with the fact that a year before, in 1149, Cadwaladr had built a powerful castle at Llanrhystud, after which he made over his portion of Ceredigion to his son Cadfan. Given the tense relationship between Hywel and his uncle, Cadwaladr, this transfer of power might have been intended to avoid provoking the seizure of the latter's share of Ceredigion; if so, it failed. Cadfan was captured along with his castle, so that by the beginning of 1150 Hywel ab Owain Gwynedd controlled the whole of Ceredigion, along with the neighbouring *cantref* of Meirionydd. This was a substantial landholding that stretched from the Teifi, in the south, to the Mawddach in the north, and it seems that Owain was complicit in the creation of this power base. Although Owain was fully engaged in campaigning against Powys and the earl of Chester during 1149–50, there is no evidence to suggest that he disapproved of, much less opposed, his son's territorial aggrandizement.

It may be significant that while one son, Hywel, was indulged by his father, another, Cynan, was set to feel his wrath. The chroniclers make no effort to explain why Owain imprisoned his younger son, though a later source does state that it was due to 'certeine faultes committed against his father'.[16] Until this point Hywel and Cynan had worked closely together but the latter's fall from grace ended the partnership and, although he was later released, it was never truly renewed. Only once more are the brothers noted in partnership, in 1159, on campaign in the south in the

'Slayers of their enemies': Owain and Cadwaladr

company of their former adversary, their uncle Cadwaladr. In view of the fact that Cynan's heirs were later associated with the lordship of Meirionydd, it is possible that the cause of his detention was a falling out with Hywel and Owain over possession of this region. The favour shown to Hywel, widely regarded as Owain's intended successor, may have led to jealousy on Cynan's part and led him to demand some territorial reward for his martial efforts. That his sons later ruled Meirionydd suggests that on his release a deal may have been struck whereby the lordship was transferred to Cynan as an apanage.

As his sons grew to manhood, Owain was faced with the prospect of satisfying their ambition for land and power. The death of Owain's (apparently) favourite son, Rhun, in 1146, left at least seven sons vying for his favour which, allied to his ongoing struggle to manage his brother, Cadwaladr, must have been a source of continuing tension within the family. That Cadwaladr had sons, perhaps as many as four, presented Owain with a further challenge but, in the event, and for reasons that remain unexplained, the latter chose to vent his spleen on the son of his deceased elder brother, Cunedda. In 1152 the author of the *Brut* relates how

> Owain ap Gruffudd caused Cunedda ap Cadwallon, his nephew, his brother's son, to be castrated and his eyes to be gouged out of his head.[17]

Unless he had committed some heinous act for which he deserved such harsh punishment, it seems that Cunedda's only crime was to be a contender for the succession, hence he was 'gelded... lest he shulde have children to enherite parte of the landes'.[18] Having disposed of his nephew,

Owain finally turned on his brother, expelling him from his last remaining stronghold, Anglesey, and thereafter exiling him from Gwynedd. Unlike the other sources, the *Cronica Wallie* offers a plausible reason to explain why events had taken such a dramatic turn:

> Aboute the same tyme dyd Cadwalader brother to Prince Owen escape out of his nevew Howelles prison, and subdued parte of the Ille of Mone or Anglesey to him. But his brother Owen sent an armye against him, and chaced him thence, and he fledde to Englande for succours to his wives frendes.[19]

The authenticity and accuracy of the *Cronica Walliae* may be a matter for debate but it should not be excluded as a source of some merit. Written in 1559 by Humphrey Llwyd, scholar, cartographer and some time Member of Parliament, the *Cronica Walliae* was based mainly on versions of the *Brut y Tywysogyon* and other unnamed sources. Therefore, there is every reason to believe that Llwyd used, and had access to, sources now lost.[20] After 1147 Cadwaladr's position in Gwynedd was, and remained, precarious and given Hywel's abrasive relationship with his uncle, it is entirely possible that he had been seized and imprisoned by his nephew. The aim, presumably, was to permanently exclude Cadwaladr and his imprisoned son, Cadfan, from their landholdings and, more importantly, from the succession.

With Ireland now closed to him, Cadwaladr had no choice but to flee to England, though he chose the baronial court of his former ally, Ranulf, earl of Chester, rather than the royal court of King Stephen. With an eye for an opportunity to avenge himself on Owain for the crushing defeat two years earlier at Coleshill, Ranulf welcomed Cadwaladr as a useful

'Slayers of their enemies': Owain and Cadwaladr

ally. An added attraction might have been the prospect of marriage with Ranulf's sister, Adeliza, widow of Richard fitzGilbert de Clare.[21] Proposing such a union in order to cement the alliance demonstrated Ranulf's commitment to Cadwaladr's cause and, of course, his own interest. Both J.E. Lloyd and Huw Pryce suggest that another reason for the marriage was to strengthen Cadwaladr's claim to Ceredigion, control of which had, by 1153, been forcibly wrested from his nephew, Hywel, by the young dynasts of Deheubarth.

It seems that Ranulf had been courting Cadwaladr as an ally for some years before he fled to his court. During the late 1140s and early 1150s, Cadwaladr regularly appears as a witness to Ranulf's charters at Haughmond Abbey near Shrewsbury.[22] In them Cadwaladr is styled king of Wales (*rege Waliarum*) and king of north Wales (*rege Nortwaliarum*) which Huw Pryce has, not unreasonably, taken to mean 'that Ranulf encouraged his ally's regal ambitions in Gwynedd so as to make trouble for Owain'.[23] Unfortunately for Cadwaladr, his hope of supplanting his brother as ruler of Gwynedd was dealt a serious blow at the end of 1153 when Earl Ranulf died. As one door closed another opened when, in 1154, King Stephen died and was succeeded by Matilda's son, Henry of Anjou. The accession of Henry II, accompanied by successful campaigns against dissident barons in the March of Wales and in France, brought the civil war in England to an end. For those who had served his mother and the Angevin cause there were rewards aplenty. For his service at the Battle of Lincoln, and doubtless for other deeds that have gone unrecorded, Henry II bestowed the manor of Ness in Shropshire on a grateful Cadwaladr.

Valued at £7 per annum, the estate was modest but more than acceptable to a fugitive would-be king of Gwynedd.[24]

A strong and unified England spelled trouble for rulers like Owain and the dynasts of Deheubarth, who had spent the best part of 20 years campaigning to win back territories lost to Norman conquest and settlement. Henry II was determined not just to reduce native power but also to restore royal authority in Wales and return it to the superior status it had enjoyed under his predecessor and namesake, Henry I. By 1157 Henry was ready to test his strength against Owain Gwynedd and with the aid of a formidable army and fleet, he marched on north Wales. Conspicuous among his Welsh supporters was Cadwaladr who commanded a troop of fellow Welshmen in the company of other native rulers such as Madog ap Maredudd of Powys and Hywel ab Ieuaf of Arwystli. The net result of the expedition was the submission of Owain and the reinstatement of Cadwaladr to his lands in Gwynedd, minus Meirionydd. If Cadwaladr had hoped for more from his service to Henry II he was to be bitterly disappointed. The expedition was a turning point in Cadwaladr's relationship with his brother. It seems that a deeper and more lasting rapprochement had taken place for Cadwaladr never again betrayed his brother and he remained steadfast in his loyalty until the latter's death in 1170. It is possible that Cadwaladr had come to realise that he would never dislodge his brother and that his allies were less interested in him than in his potential to do Owain harm. When Cadwaladr realised his folly and how easily he had been manipulated by Henry II, he finally accepted the, not ungenerous, settlement his brother was disposed to offer him. In effect, Cadwaladr was taken back on terms that

'Slayers of their enemies': Owain and Cadwaladr

suggest he had accepted that he must become a 'feudatory' of his brother whom he acknowledged to be his overlord in a unified kingdom.

Although ruthless in his treatment of disloyalty or rivalry – witness the imprisoning of one son and the mutilation of a nephew – Owain showed a remarkable capacity for deceiving himself about his brother, and an astonishing indulgence of his most patent duplicity. Cadwaladr was never threatened with mutilation or death, and although he was periodically deprived of land and exiled, he was almost as frequently pardoned and restored. Whether this was due, in part, to what Sean Davies believes was a significant 'development in chivalric attitudes' is a matter for debate.[25] What is certain is that the mutilation of a young man, Cunedda, a punishment widely practised in Wales and elsewhere at this time, suggests that thoughts of a less chivalrous nature were influencing Owain in his treatment of potentially hostile members of his extended family. In the final analysis, Cadwaladr was a prominent personage throughout his brother's reign but, in a rather cutting assessment, J.E. Lloyd opined that 'Cadwladar was the ordinary, as Owain was the exceptional', being no more than a 'foil to the greatness of Owain'.[26]

V

A test of strength: Owain and Henry II

> He overflowed the bounds of ordinary men's comprehension. He bewildered them with his contradictory qualities. He baffled them by his disregard of contemporary wisdom. He astonished them by his tireless energy and resilience. He attempted the impossible and achieved the improbable.[1]

IF LEWIS WARREN'S ASSESSMENT of Henry of Anjou is accurate, and we have no reason to doubt it, he was clearly an extraordinary man and one to be reckoned with. His accession to the throne of England in October 1154 changed the political landscape. Within two years the warring factions that had contributed to the so-called 'anarchy' of Stephen's reign had been reduced to submission so that by 1157, Henry II was ready to deal with Wales. Henry II was to prove a formidable adversary and Owain needed to harness and utilize every scrap of wit and cunning he had at his disposal.

Kings of England had long claimed lordship over Wales. Their aim, primarily, was the submission of their Celtic

A test of strength: Owain and Henry II

neighbours, the native rulers, from whom they sought to elicit at least an acknowledgement of the English Crown's superior status or, failing that, the means to reduce the Welsh to obedience. At no point before the campaigns of the last quarter of the thirteenth century, did either Saxon, Norman or English kings seriously contemplate the total conquest and annexation of Wales. Domination and submission, rather than conquest and assimilation, were the twin themes that underpinned royal policy towards the Welsh. For their part, the Welsh rulers seem not to have objected unduly to either submitting or acknowledging the will of the English Crown, their objective always to retain the initiative in native affairs and, as far as possible, to maintain their personal and political independence, as much from each other as from the English king. This called for a delicate and deferential balancing act, a *modus vivendi* between the wearers of the English crown and Welsh coronet, the success of which depended more on the Welsh than the English. Indeed, if the Welsh were to succeed they needed to possess and exhibit in equal measure the characteristics ascribed to the Lord Rhys ap Gruffudd of Deheubarth at his death in 1197, namely 'a Ulysses for speech, a Solomon for wisdom, an Ajax for mind, and the foundation of all accomplishments!'.[2] That few of the native rulers measured up to the exacting standards set by Rhys's annalistic admirers, might explain why the relationship between English kings and Welsh princes was, more realistically, marked as much by violence, vitriol and vindictiveness as by accommodation, accomplishment and agreement.

Among the more talented native rulers who may be counted the equal of the Lord Rhys was Owain Gwynedd.

65

For two decades he had turned to his advantage the collapse of the 'delicate and deferential balancing act' that had marked Stephen's reign. During this period of native resurgence, labelled in rather grandiose terms by J.E. Lloyd as 'The National Revival', much of the land lost to the first and second generation of Norman adventurers and conquistadors had been won back mainly by blood, battle, tears and sweat. Now all they had to do was keep hold of their gains. As R.R. Davies eloquently put it:

> Expansion was just as necessary as consolidation for the political and economic well-being of a native Welsh principality. It was thus that its resources in men, plunder, and power were augmented, the momentum and ambitions of its war-bands sustained, and the bulwarks built to protect its heartland.[3]

Almost as soon as he became king, Henry II set down a marker that spelled trouble for Owain and his fellow Welsh rulers. Reflecting on his kingship, Henry is reported to have said:

> When by God's favour I attained the kingdom of England, I resumed many things which had been dispersed and alienated from the royal demesne in the time of Stephen my usurper.[4]

Unlike his Norman predecessors, Henry hailed from Anjou, a region of France south of Normandy, and his territorial concerns were much wider than theirs. He became the ruler of a vast 'Empire', so-called because it covered the greater part of France and the British Isles and consisted of a number of quite separate and independent territories of which the principalities of Wales formed but a small, almost insignificant, part. That said, Henry was forced to spend a

A test of strength: Owain and Henry II

proportionately greater amount of time and energy in dealing with affairs in Wales than any of his kingly predecessors had done. This was due in no small measure to the spirited and independently-minded princes, led by Owain, who resisted their Angevin neighbour at every turn. Their will to resist stemmed in part from the success they had enjoyed at the expense of their Anglo-Norman neighbours who, on account of the inability of the Crown under Stephen to support them, were flung on the defensive. Although not as chaotic a reign as was once thought, there is no doubt that as a result of the civil war between Stephen and the supporters of the late king's daughter, Matilda, the Crown had neither the time nor the resources, nor indeed the will, to maintain, in any meaningful sense, its overlordship in Wales. Consequently, this resurgence in native power – the expansion and strengthening of Gwynedd, the stabilisation of Powys and the re-emergence of Deheubarth – inevitably impacted on the Crown in so far as native-controlled Wales or *pura Wallia* expanded while the Anglo-Norman March or *marchia Wallie* contracted.

There is no doubt that the Anglo-Normans had suffered a serious setback in their attempts to subdue and settle substantial parts of Wales. Equally, the Welsh recovery was deeply rooted and 'more than simply the swing of the military pendulum'.[5] The reclamation of lands lost prior to Stephen's reign by the dynasts of Gwynedd was extensive, but the real test of strength was in holding on to them in the face of a resurgent English Crown. By 1157 Owain had been in power for 20 years, time enough perhaps to expand, consolidate and firmly establish his power and hegemony. However, the reality was rather starker: he had to manage disappointment and dissension within his own family while combating Anglo-Norman and native enemies on Gwynedd's borders. War had been a constant theme throughout his kingship and while he might have been able to consolidate, develop and more firmly establish his authority in those areas of the kingdom largely untouched by continuing conflict, mainly Gwynedd Uwch Conwy, his hold on the peripheral parts of his realm was altogether more tenuous. Gwynedd Is Conwy, especially Tegeingl, Dyffryn Clwyd and Ystrad Alun, was vulnerable to attack as, to a lesser extent, was Meirionydd, whilst Ceredigion had been lost entirely to the resurgent dynasty of Deheubarth by 1153. There was a precariousness to Owain's success and achievements which, according to R.R. Davies, was 'cruelly exposed by Henry II in 1157–8'.[6]

It is perhaps fair to say that given Henry's ignorance of Wales and Welsh affairs prior to his accession, he may be said to have blundered onto the scene in the mid-1150s determined, it seems, to reduce the princes to a position of servile dependence. Thus, when war came in 1157, the mechanisms designed to regulate and arbitrate the relationship between the king of England and the prince of Gwynedd had hardly been exhausted, but both sides seem to have been overcome by a sense of the inevitability of conflict. In July, Henry met his nobility to plan the campaign against the Welsh and within weeks the king had 'led a mighty host to Chester, in order to subdue Gwynedd'.[7] In response Owain summoned 'to him his sons and his leading men, and gathering together a mighty host, encamped at Basingwerk... there to give battle to the king'.[8]

A test of strength: Owain and Henry II

The pretext for invasion was provided by the exiled Cadwaladr who, according to Lewis Warren

> was a suppliant at Henry's court, claiming that he had been deprived of his rightful inheritance; and it is likely that it suited Henry's purpose to assert the overlordship he claimed in defence of a Welshman's rights rather than in support of dispossessed [Anglo-Norman] settlers.[9]

This was a propaganda coup for Henry who used it to the full, for in publicly supporting Cadwaladr he was also highlighting the fact that the Welshman had rendered useful service to the Angevin cause during the civil war. In reality the main reason for the invasion was to reduce to submission 'the most powerful as well as the most truculent of the Welsh rulers'.[10] A subdued and pliant Owain would send a powerful message to those Welsh rulers, such as the Lord Rhys, who were contemplating resisting the Crown. Engineered by Henry or not, there was no stopping him once the preparations for invasion had been set in motion.

The plan of attack was two-fold: a landward invasion led by Henry II, supported by an offshore fleet which later sailed to ravage Anglesey and disrupt Owain's line of retreat. If Henry thought the sight of an impressively large and well-organised army, the first royal expedition to enter Wales since 1121, would encourage Owain to submit, he was wrong. The Welsh stood their ground and prepared to meet the enemy in battle near Basingwerk. Whether this surprised Henry and caused him to change tactics is not known, but he resolved to outflank the Welsh by executing a risky manoeuvre that called for a mobile, lightly-armed troop to plunge into the forest west of Owain's army. Advancing with 'more dash than prudence', according to the chronicler Gervase of Canterbury, Henry quickly found himself in serious difficulty.[11] Anticipating such a move, Owain had dispatched his sons, Dafydd and Cynan, with forces large enough to patrol the dense forest and crush any force foolish enough to fight the Welsh on their own terms. As masters of guerrilla warfare, the Welsh were used to operating on such challenging terrain, whilst the Anglo-Normans were simply not equipped to cope with the difficult conditions they encountered. In the wood at Coleshill near Hawarden, the royal troop was cut to pieces and in the ensuing melée Henry's close companions, Eustace fitzJohn, constable of Chester Castle, and Robert de Courcy, were killed, whilst his standard bearer, Henry of Essex, fled in panic. The native chroniclers relate how the Welsh had given Henry 'a severe battle. And after many of the king's men had been slain, it was with difficulty that he escaped'.[12] In the opinion of one Welsh chronicler, it was Dafydd ab Owain Gwynedd who deserved the credit for this victory for he not only 'pursued them', he was 'slaughtering them murderously' as he did so.[13]

Doubtless shocked by his close encounter with death, Henry pressed on regardless and continued the campaign. In the face of overwhelming force, Owain retreated, first to St Asaph and then to Rhuddlan, all the while pursued by the royal army. When Henry reached Rhuddlan, news filtered through of the disaster that had befallen his fleet. Putting into Moelfre, the troops disembarked from the ships and proceeded to pillage the villages and churches in the vicinity. Their complacency was such that they were ill prepared to resist the onslaught that was visited upon them the following

A test of strength: Owain and Henry II

day by the 'men of Anglesey', during which battle, in the words of the native chroniclers

> the French… fled and some of them were captured, others were slain, others were drowned, and it was only with difficulty that a few of them escaped back to the ships, after Henry, son of king Henry [I], and all the chief seamen, for the greater part, had been slain.[14]

Gerald of Wales too wrote of the disaster which he claimed was God's punishment for the sacking of 'holy places throughout the island' which is why 'the islanders won a bloody victory'.[15] Henry's first expedition to Wales must have been a sobering experience for the Angevin for it was not long ere he and Owain agreed terms for a truce. It is not known who made the first move to sue for peace but it was likely the Welshman who sought out the Angevin. Owain was no fool and he must have come to realise that, but for the setbacks that befell Henry, the forces arrayed against him had the potential to crush him. Owain was compelled to do homage to Henry, acknowledge his suzerainty, give hostages as pledges for his future conduct, reinstate Cadwaladr and give up Tegeingl. In the opinion of a contemporary Norman chronicler, Robert de Toringy, the king had 'subjected the Welsh to his will' though the truth was rather more complex; Owain had been humbled but not humiliated, he had made his submission but was not subdued.[16]

Although largely effected by military means, the 'humbling' of Owain was accomplished as much by political as by economic forces. The Crown was always able to exploit the deep divisions in Welsh political life and make the most of family disunity, particularly as it affected landed inheritance and the issue of succession. Thus was Owain's brother Cadwaladr courted and won over to the English cause. Nor were the other native rulers of Powys and Deheubarth able to resist, periodically, the temptation of benefitting from the king's considerable wealth and bounty and in so doing effectively detaching them from the belligerent elements threatening the power of the king, Henry II. It was, in the words of Rees Davies, 'domination by munificence', since the contents of Owain's coffers could not match those at the disposal of the king even one who spent generously, as Henry II did, in pursuit of his ambitions.[17]

Henceforward, Owain exercised caution in his dealings with Henry II, always stopping short of provoking the king. He showed great restraint, even in the face of provocation by the Crown and its allies. No sooner had Henry left north Wales than Owain was attacked by Iorwerth Goch, brother of Madog ap Maredudd, ruler of Powys. The attack centred on the castle Owain had erected at Tomen y Rhodwydd in 1149 to secure the commote of Iâl. The castle was taken and destroyed, and the commote recovered by the victorious men of Powys. As Owain suffered this rebuff at the hands of Henry's allies, he had to endure the indignity of witnessing the re-building of three fortresses by the Crown, at Rhuddlan, Prestatyn and Basingwerk, which were designed to secure and protect Tegeingl. Henry was soon drawn to his continental possessions, and the conduct of royal policy in England as well as Wales was entrusted to his justiciars, Richard de Lucy and Robert de Beaumont, earl of Leicester.

In biding his time, Owain had occasionally to enter

A test of strength: Owain and Henry II

into an unwilling partnership with his erstwhile foes, as in 1159, when the full weight of royal authority was directed towards subduing the ruler of Deheubarth, the Lord Rhys. Presumably acting on the instructions of the king's justiciars, the royal army that invaded south-west Wales was led by Reginald, earl of Cornwall, the illegitimate son of Henry I. Owain was obliged to send forces under the command of his sons Hywel and Cynan, alongside those more willingly provided by Cadwaladr who joined his nephews and Reginald's Anglo-Norman army in operations against Rhys ap Gruffudd. In 1160 Owain again demonstrated his fidelity to the bargain struck with Henry when he delivered Einion Clud, who had been captured and imprisoned by his brother Cadwallon ap Madog of Maelienydd, to Crown officials who promptly threw him into the gaol at Worcester Castle: but from which he later escaped.

By 1162 Owain's patience was running out and when Hywel ab Ieuaf launched an unprovoked attack on the lordship of Cyfeiliog, taking by storm its castle of Tafolwern, he felt compelled to act. Hywel was driven out of Cyfeiliog and was pursued to his lordship of Arwystli which was ravaged by forces led by Owain himself. Though he was a man of ripening years, Owain had lost none of his flair for battle and in the midst of a counter-attack he

> urged his men to fight. And the enemies turned to flight, with Owain and his men slaughtering them, so that hardly a third part of them escaped home in flight.[18]

Fortunately for Owain, the Crown did not react to this aggressive show of force in a region, Cyfeiliog and Arwystli, the north Welshmen had no business interfering in. It may be that Owain had set himself the task of taking advantage of the civil strife besetting Powys following the death of Madog ap Maredudd in 1160. Cyfeiliog was ripe for annexation, as were other more peripheral parts of Powys, particularly those bordering Gwynedd. With the warring sons of Madog ap Maredudd and the Lord Rhys also flexing their military muscle, as much against each other as against the alien settlers, Henry was induced to return from the continent and mount another expedition to pacify the Welsh.

The focus of this latest pacification policy was not Owain Gwynedd but the Lord Rhys. Almost as soon as Henry set foot in south Wales, Rhys realised the scale of the task confronting him and although he considered resisting he was, according to Gerald of Wales, dissuaded from doing so by Owain.[19] Following Owain's advice, Rhys surrendered to Henry and accompanied him to England. However, if Owain thought this was the end of the matter and that he would be left in peace, if not rewarded for his timely intervention, he was mistaken. The tried and tested mechanisms and rituals of submission – military campaigns followed by parleys, pledges, hostages and tribute – had been pursued with vigour but Henry wished to settle the 'Welsh question' by adopting a potentially innovative conciliar approach to the problem. Thus, sometime prior to 1 July 1163, Owain was summoned to meet the king and his council at Woodstock. He was not alone. In the words of one who witnessed the gathering, Ralph of Diceto:

> Malcolm king of the Scots, Rhys prince of the southern Welsh, Owain of the northern, and five of the greater men of Wales did homage to the king of England and to Henry his son.[20]

A test of strength: Owain and Henry II

Woodstock was the first of four councils held between 1163 and 1177 (the others were held at Gloucester in 1175, Geddington and Oxford in 1177), each of which was devoted almost exclusively to Welsh affairs – an innovation in itself – and each was attended by a gathering of native princes, Marcher barons and royal councillors. They were clearly intended to be great state occasions attended by the usual formalities and ceremonial that one might expect when the king was sitting amidst his senior councillors without whom he was apparently unwilling to act. In bringing together the rulers of *pura Wallia* and *marchia Wallie* the king was seeking consensus in delineating more clearly the limit and extent of their respective territorial and, to a lesser degree, political power while, at the same time, defining more closely his authority over them. According to Lewis Warren, at Woodstock Owain and his compatriots were 'required to demean themselves by accepting instead of their previous client status that of dependent vassalage'.[21]

It was this apparent redefinition of their terms of allegiance that roused Owain and his fellow rulers to anger and indignation, for in forcing them to swear homage the king was, it seems, demanding more than the usual (and by this date routine) oaths of fealty. In a society based on personal dependence, subordination need not necessarily imply humiliation and powerlessness in either theory or practice. In rendering oaths of fealty – a personal oath of loyalty from a vassal to his lord – the princes had long ago accepted a subordinate position in their relationship with the Crown which did not, apparently, necessitate either grants of territory or incur other related 'feudal' incidents. That such grants had occurred and that some 'feudal incidents' were incurred serves only to obscure what was, in essence, an arrangement between individual kings and their native vassals. The intensity, complexity or elasticity of those relationships between the individuals concerned varied enormously over time and according to circumstance.

However, in the ceremony associated with homage, the princes might have been expected to bind themselves so rigidly to the king that they would have entered into a 'feudal' framework familiar to the Crown and its English and continental tenants but largely alien to themselves. True, the Welsh were not unfamiliar with the terminology and rituals associated with submission and which were as much a part of their social structure as those found in so-called 'feudal' England or France; but that Henry II is acknowledged to have sought a firmer definition of his overlordship which was, in the words of Rees Davies, 'novel in its precision and demeaning in its character', suggests that much of what he intended was indeed alien and unpalatable to the princes.[22] They would have become vassals of the Crown, pledging to render whatever service had been specified or was customary at the time. In submitting to the will and authority of successive English kings, Owain's ancestors had helped to establish a pattern of political dominance and dependence with which the Crown was well satisfied. Owain's ambitions however challenged and threatened this relationship which the Crown held to be unacceptable. The Crown, for its part, moulded and exploited history and tradition in its favour, and by the second half of the twelfth century the idea that Wales and its ruler(s) were in some way tied and beholden to the king, and had always been so, was accepted as fact. It was a misrepresentation of the facts and a carefully planned

A test of strength: Owain and Henry II

manipulation of the truth, but it held sway simply because it was written by, and eventually enshrined in, the political code of the strongest power.

Unfortunately, only Ralph of Diceto and Robert of Torigny provide accounts of the assembly at Woodstock, and neither is forthcoming on the precise details attending the oaths rendered. Despite this, it is worth speculating on what transpired at Woodstock inasmuch as it seems to have caused the princes to set aside their bitter rivalry and unite in the face of what they perceived to be an ominous and common threat. It was usual for those rendering homage – the ceremonial acceptance of inferiority to a lord as a precondition for taking possession of land as his feudal tenant – to be publicly enfeoffed with property on pain of forfeiture if they failed in their duty to their feudal overlord. If Henry II intended that the princes' patrimonies, their kingdoms as opposed to any additional lands, were to be included in this public enfeoffment, this would have all but admitted the king's right to direct territorial lordship over each of them. If this was the case then it would have heralded a major shift in policy since, hitherto, the princes had not formally held their lands of this or any other king of England; their dependence on the royal incumbent had been personal, not territorial.

That this is what the king intended may be suggested by his treatment in 1158 of the Lord Rhys whom he stripped of his territories before 'his being allowed *Cantref Mawr* and another *cantref*, which the king chose to give him, and that whole and not divided'.[23] That Henry did not keep to his promise 'but gave him various portions within the lands of various barons' indicated early the danger he posed to the princes.[24] In fact, contemporaries who knew Henry were not surprised since he was widely acknowledged to be an oath-breaker. In a letter to the bishop of Ostia, Henry's former friend, Archbishop Thomas Becket, stated that 'in slipperiness he outdid Proteus'.[25] Gerald of Wales, too, was scathing about the king saying that 'he was always ready to break his word', while the anonymous author of the French chronicle, *Historia gloriosi Regis Ludovici VII*, refers to Henry's 'accustomed trickery in the manner of a deceitful fox'.[26]

Owain did not trust Henry or his motives, probably with good reason, and was perhaps among the first to realise the implications of what the king was demanding. This might explain why he decided to throw caution to the wind and rise against the Angevin. His fellow rulers, it seems, shared his concern and they did not need much persuading to join him in making war on the king. In a remarkable show of unity, and with Owain at their head, the Welsh determined to throw off 'the bondage of the French'.[27] The first into the field was the Lord Rhys when, in 1164, he attacked the Anglo-Norman settlements in Ceredigion. Within months Owain too had joined the fray when, early in 1165, his son Dafydd launched an attack on Tegeingl. It has been suggested that the spark that lit the flame of conflict in Wales was Henry's quarrel with his chancellor and Archbishop, Thomas Becket. True, the two had seriously fallen out leading to the flight abroad of Becket in October 1164, but the current consensus is that the events were coincidental and that the king's difficulties with his Archbishop of Canterbury were of peripheral interest to the Welsh rulers.

It was the news of Dafydd ab Owain Gwynedd's attack on the royal castles in Tegeingl that roused Henry to action.

A test of strength: Owain and Henry II

According to Lewis Warren, Henry 'could not abide that his will be flouted, his authority impugned, or his trust abused', nor could he 'abide betrayal – or what he took to be betrayal'.[28] Owain had sworn an oath at Woodstock which he had broken and, worse, he had attacked and taken castles belonging to the Crown. To Henry, this made the conflict personal and, if the native chroniclers are to be believed, in his anger the king 'gathered a host beyond number of the picked warriors of England and Normandy and Flanders and Gascony and Anjou and all the North and Scotland'; his aim was 'to annihilate all Welshmen'.[29]

After an initial foray into north Wales, in May 1165, perhaps to ease the pressure on his hard-pressed garrisons and to revive their flagging morale, Henry returned to England to prepare for what would, arguably, be the largest invasion force ever assembled by a king of England.

In an impressive show of force that included contingents from Powys, Deheubarth and Gwynedd, the Welsh awaited Henry's invading army at Corwen. If Henry hoped the size and scale of the royal army might cause the Welsh to seek terms, he was to be deeply disappointed. Emboldened by the scale of their own unified forces and inspired by the leadership of Owain Gwynedd, the Welsh remained steadfast in their determination to rout the invading enemy. According to Gervase of Canterbury, the Welsh harried the invading troops as they struggled to cope with the terrain, first in the forests of the Ceiriog Valley and then on the bog-laden hills of the Berwyn. The logistics involved in leading, organising and supplying such a large force must have been formidable. The native chroniclers stated quite unequivocally that the supply of food was proving to be particularly difficult which, allied to the effects of unseasonal weather, did much to sap the morale of Henry's army.[30] Although it was mid-August, the high winds and torrential rain had, according to Paul Latimer, 'turned the uplands into a bitterly cold quagmire'.[31] Henry, it seems, was losing more men to starvation and exposure than to enemy action. Curiously, the Anglo-Norman chronicler, William of Newburgh, who had waxed lyrical on Henry's triumphant campaign of 1157, had little to say on this occasion, other than to suggest that the king's expedition had been a success.[32]

In truth, Henry's campaign had been an abject failure, 'the greatest defeat of his career' according to David Carpenter, and the king's ill-tempered reaction in killing and maiming his Welsh hostages in retribution indicate that he thought so too.[33] Owain's sons, Rhys and Cadwallon, were among those hostages who escaped death but had their eyes gouged out instead. Henry was loath to leave the field of conflict and let the Welsh go unpunished, which is perhaps why he resolved upon a plan of campaign that had been used before, in 1157, of combining the operations of his army with a fleet. Although it had met with only limited success, Henry clearly had faith in the principle of the plan and thought that if it was better co-ordinated and executed it had the potential to crush the Welsh. Unfortunately for him, the Hiberno-Scandinavian fleet he hired from Dublin arrived well short of the shipping he had envisaged and which he thought necessary for the plan to succeed. Bitterly disappointed, he paid the Irish off and they returned to Ireland. It is perhaps significant that the Dubliners had contracted with Henry rather than their usual allies, the Welsh, which may have had something to

Maps and Pedigrees

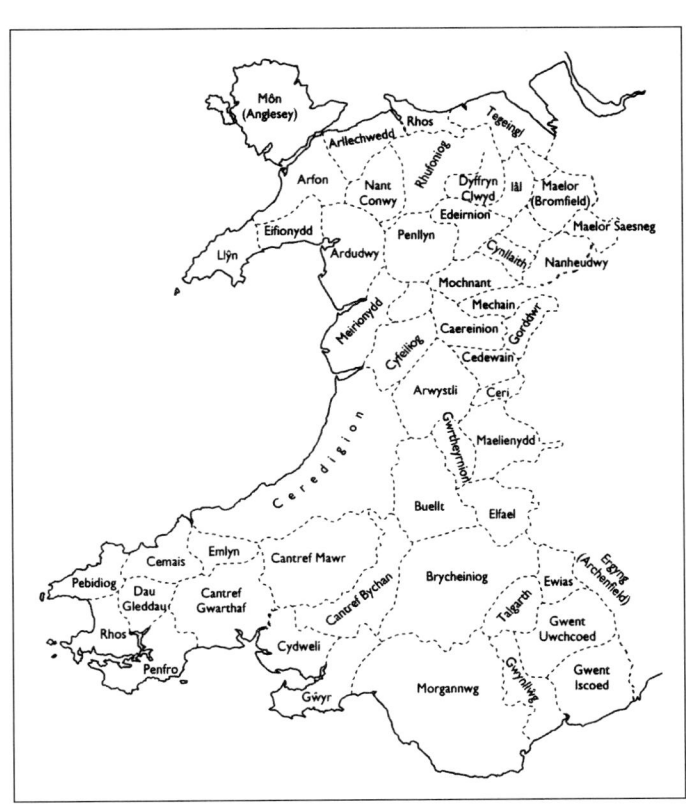

1. Regional and Local Divisions of Medieval Wales.

2. Gwynedd c.1105. The kingdom of Gwynedd early in the reign of Gruffudd ap Cynan.

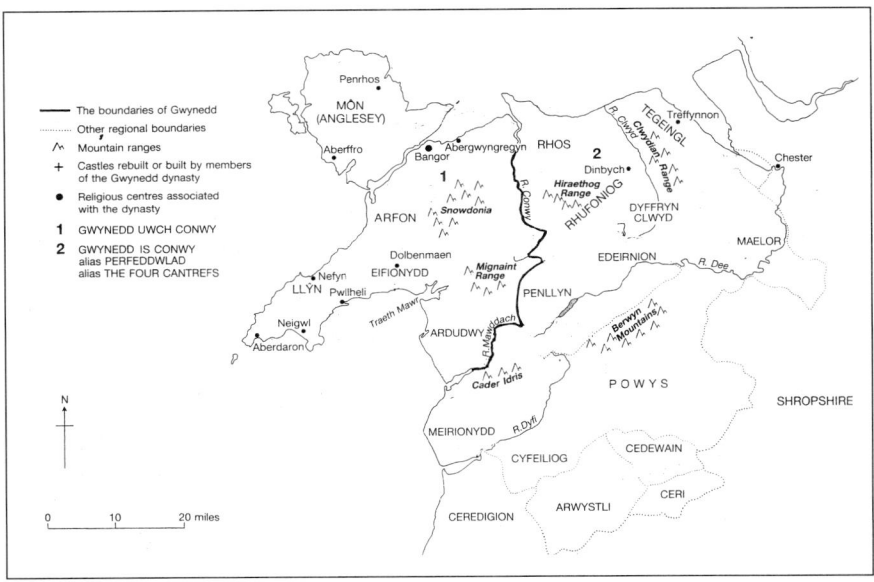

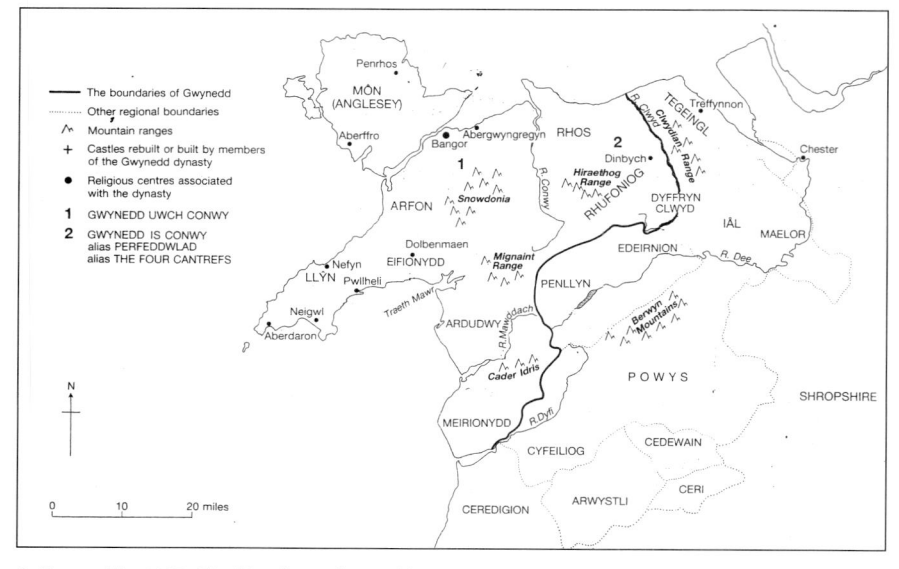

3. Gwynedd c.1137. The kingdom inherited by Owain Gwynedd.

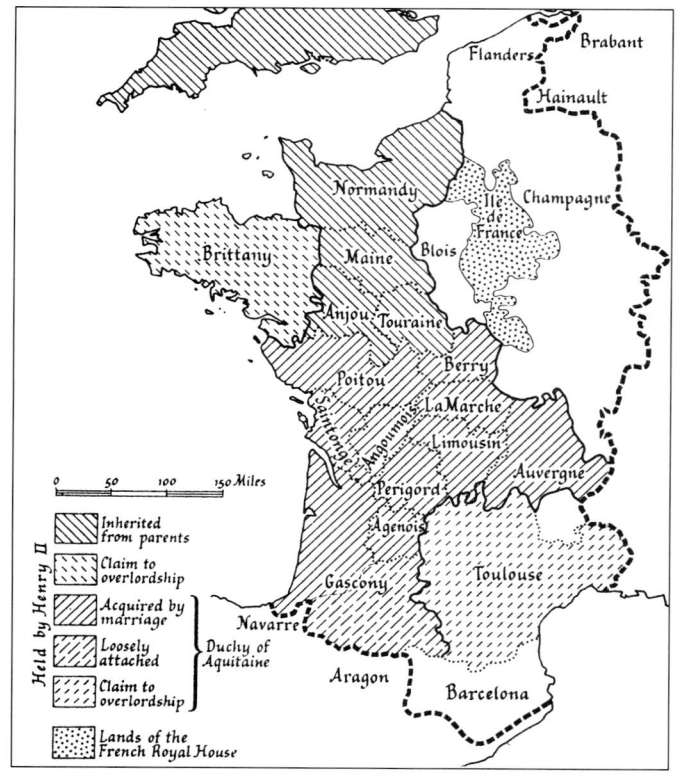

4. France and the Angevin Empire c.1160s. The continental possessions of King Henry II of England and the territory of King Louis VII of France.

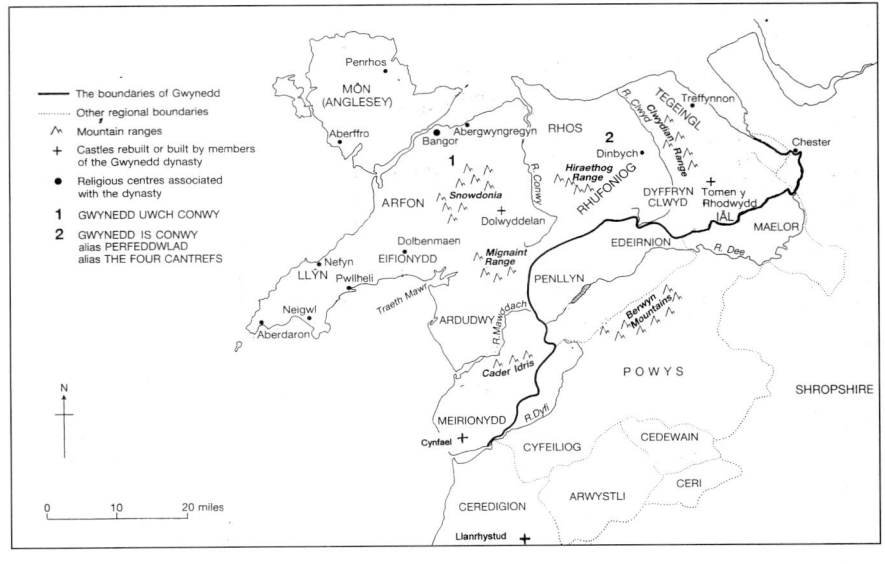

5. Gwynedd c.1170. The extent of the kingdom of Gwynedd at Owain's death.

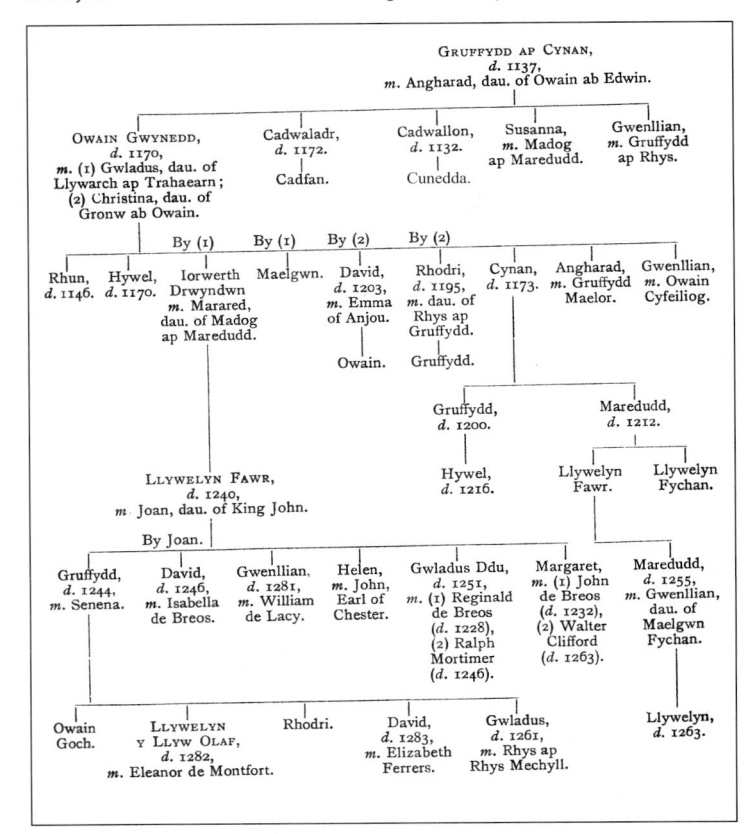

6. The Dynasty of Gwynedd.

Illustrations

1. Artist's impression of Owain Gwynedd. This imaginary portrait of Owain Gwynedd was painted by Hugh Williams in 1909.

Reproduced by kind permission of the National Library of Wales

2. Coat of arms attributed to Owain Gwynedd in the choir stalls of Bangor Cathedral. The coat of arms attributed to Owain Gwynedd can be dated no earlier than the fifteenth century. However, the near contemporary court poets, Cynddelw Brydydd Mawr and Llywarch ap Llywelyn, make reference to Owain Gwynedd as the ruler of Eryri (the land of eagles). The shield is thought to have been installed in the 1960s.

Photograph by David R. Price

3. Castell Tomen y Rhodwydd. Erected in 1149 by Owain Gywnedd, Tomen y Rhodwydd is one of the largest motte and bailey castles in north Wales.
© Crown Copyright: Royal Commission on the Ancient and Historical Monuments of Wales

4. Castell Cynfael. Built by Cadwaladr ap Gruffudd, Cynfael castle was besieged and destroyed in 1147.
© Crown Copyright: Royal Commission on the Ancient and Historical Monuments of Wales

5. Llanrhystud Castle. Built by Cadwaladr ap Gruffudd in 1149, Llanrhystud castle was besieged and taken in 1150.
© Crown Copyright: Royal Commission on the Ancient and Historical Monuments of Wales

6. Early fourteenth-century manuscript depiction of Henry II and Thomas Becket. The manuscript shows King Henry II arguing with Archbishop Thomas Becket. Becket was murdered by Henry's knights in 1170.
© British Library

7. The stone tablet erected to mark the burial place of Owain Gwynedd in Bangor Cathedral. Mr David R. Price believes it may have been laid prior to the refurbishment of the cathedral by Gilbert Scott in 1870.

Transcription of Memorial to Owain Gwynedd
The body which lies interred within this wall in a stone coffin, is supposed to be the remains of OWEN GWYNEDD Sovereign Prince of Wales, he reigned 32 years, and died A.D. 1169, both this Prince, and his brother CADWALLADER, were buried in this Cathedral Church. History represents them as highly distinguished for courage, humanity, and courteous manners. Their father, GRIFFITH ap CYNAN, the last sovereign, known by the title King of Wales overthrew TRAHAERN ap CARADOC, and ascended the throne of his ancestors, A.D. 1079, he was afterwards taken by treachery and imprisoned in the Castle at Chester, 12 years, he escaped, recovered the entire possession of his Kingdom, reigned 57 years, and died in his 83rd year, he was buried near the/ Great Altar, which with the larger part of the fabrick, was destroyed during the insurrection of OWEN GLYNDWR, about A.D. 1404, the present church was erected about A.D. 1496, by HENRY DEAN, who was at that time Bishop of the Diocese, Lord Justice and Lord Chancellor of Ireland, and in A.D. 1500 Bishop of Salisbury and in A.D. 1501, Archbishop of Canterbury.
Photograph and transcription by David R. Price

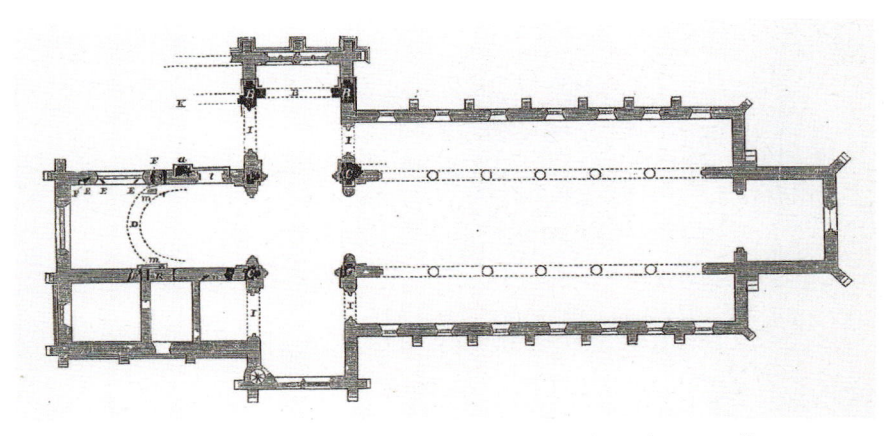

8. Plan of Bangor Cathedral drawn up by Gilbert Scott in 1870. It shows the original location, prior to their removal and relocation, of the remains of two tombs thought to be those of Owain Gwynedd and Gruffudd ap Cynan.
Plan supplied by David R. Price

9. The image of a Welsh king on a page from *Cyfraith Hywel*, the law of Hywel. The lawbooks that bear Hywel Dda's name can be dated no earlier than the second quarter of the thirteenth century but the manuscripts contain law which is of twelfth century origin and may have been used by rulers such as Owain Gwynedd.

National Library of Wales, Peniarth MS 28 f.1v.

10. The images of Welsh kings on a page taken from a fifteenth-century manuscript written on parchment probably in north Wales. The text is that of Geoffrey of Monmouth's *Historia Regum Britanniae* ('History of the Kings of Britain'), translated into Welsh as 'Brut y Brenhinedd' ('History of the Kings'). Geoffrey was a contemporary of Owain Gwynedd and his *Historia* was written in c.1135.

National Library of Wales, Peniarth MS 23C f.13r.

A test of strength: Owain and Henry II

do with the harsh way Owain and Cadwaladr had treated their kinsmen some two decades before, in 1144.

After his ignominious defeat, Henry left England for the continent, leaving his Marcher barons and justiciars to cope with the Welsh as best they could. Royal policy had turned from offence to defence; henceforth containment, rather than campaign, was the means by which the Crown sought to deal with the 'Welsh question'. Henry had his apologists, chroniclers such as Ralph of Coggeshall who, in spite of evidence to the contrary, claimed that the king had 'conquered the Welsh, always rebels of the kings of England' though in doing so he had suffered the 'great loss of his leading men and expenditure of his army'.[34] With due respect to the abbot of Coggeshall, Henry can hardly be said to have 'subjugated the unwilling' Welsh.[35] The difficulty of campaigning in Wales was well known to those born and bred in the March which is why Gerald of Wales was more critical of Henry, whom he blamed for the failure of the expedition

> because he placed no confidence in the local leaders, who were experienced and familiar with the conditions, preferring to take advice from men who lived far away from the Marches and knew nothing of the habits and customs of the inhabitants.[36]

In truth, Henry II had achieved no less, and certainly no more, than his kingly predecessors in so far as his authority was mediated through client rulers who took it upon themselves either to enforce or dilute his commands. The sheer scale of his territorial interests meant that Wales would always be peripheral to his other political concerns, which might explain the often rather fitful and apparently ad hoc way in which he dealt with the problems associated with native political ambitions. Preoccupied he may have been, but negligent he was not, and even though he did not return to England for four years, he had recovered his composure sufficiently to shape royal policy towards the Welsh even if it was conducted from a distance. It is noteworthy that within months of Henry's retreat, the coalition of Welsh rulers broke up and some of them returned to fighting each other. Owain and Rhys ap Gruffudd remained allies, but the ambitious and quarrelsome members of the dynasty of Powys went their own way. Indeed, ever alert to the possibilities of interfering in Welsh affairs, Henry made an ally of Owain Cyfeiliog who thereby became an enemy of Owain Gwynedd whom he fought, aided by troops supplied by the Crown, for control of the lordship of Caereinion.

In stark contrast to Henry II's experience, the campaign of 1165 had been a triumph for Owain Gwynedd, and although the weather had come to his aid, his boldness, courage and resolute leadership had impressed and inspired in equal measure. Owain did not rest on his laurels; instead he stepped up the campaign against the Anglo-Normans. In 1166 Basingwerk Castle was taken and destroyed, followed by the biggest prize of all, the castle of Rhuddlan. After a three-month siege, Rhuddlan fell in 1167, following which the lordship of Tegeingl, and presumably the castle at Prestatyn, fell into Owain's hands. Powys too came in for special attention, though his attempts to annex permanently substantial parts of the fragmented kingdom met with limited success. Nevertheless, by 1168 Owain was at the height of his power; he had seen off the threat

A test of strength: Owain and Henry II

posed by the Crown, had recovered land lost to the Anglo-Normans and, by the annexation of Tegeingl, had pushed the bounds of his kingdom almost to the very gates of Chester on the Dee.

VI

'Faithful and devoted friends': Owain and Louis VII

> Since I have heard of the magnificence of your virtue and the very eminent excellence of your dignity and nobility from the announcement of rumour and the truthful report of many; I have for a long time desired with the greatest desire to come to the notice of your highness and have your very delightful friendship.[1]

Thus did *Owinus, rex Wallie* or Owain, king of Wales, announce himself in the first of three surviving letters addressed to the king of France, Louis VII. The letter makes plain Owain Gwynedd's desire to obtain Louis's 'delightful friendship' which, in reality, was polite diplomatic speak for concluding an alliance. In what otherwise might be regarded as an unremarkable letter, an exemplar of the kind of diplomatic contacts that occurred as a matter of routine between western European heads of state, Owain's communication with the French court is one of enormous significance for the history of Wales. As far as is known, this represented the first attempt by a Welsh ruler to

'Faithful and devoted friends': Owain and Louis VII

make contact, and establish diplomatic relations, with a continental monarch. This would mark out Owain as a ruler of rare insight and ability. He was clearly a man who had an outward-looking policy, someone who wished to broaden his horizons and who wished to avail himself of opportunities, as yet untapped. In undertaking this diplomatic initiative, Owain was ably demonstrating his appreciation of the wider political and strategic situation in so far as it affected his nemesis, Henry II, and, ultimately, himself.

It has been suggested that it was Henry's attempt to make real and tangible his overlordship in Wales that spurred Owain Gwynedd into seeking an alternative overlord in the representative of the royal house of Capet, Louis VII. Certainly Owain was left suitably unimpressed, if not a little resentful, by the oath of homage he had been compelled to make at Woodstock in July 1163. Within four months of the meeting, in October 1163, Owain is said to have adopted a new title without consulting his overlord, Henry II. In a letter to Pope Alexander III, Archbishop Thomas Becket informed him about 'the Welsh and Owain, who calls himself prince' with the result that 'the lord king is very moved and offended'.[2] This was a significant move on Owain's part and the reasons for it are a matter for debate, but one thing is certain, Henry II regarded his use of the title 'prince' as an expression of defiance. Whereas Sean Duffy suggests that Owain adopted this new style simply 'to put Henry's nose out of joint', Huw Pryce argues that in assuming the title of 'prince' Owain was 'implicitly rejecting royal overlordship'.[3] J. Beverley Smith believes that the change in style, the deliberate dropping of king or *rex* in favour of prince or *princeps*, was 'intended to reflect his unquestioned eminence as the leader of his nation'.[4] If true then it may be argued that Owain was perhaps guilty of nothing more than attempting to establish his pre-eminence over his fellow Welsh rulers, rather than snub Henry II. However, even if this were the intention, any act that signalled an elevation of Owain's status would be of concern to his overlord. Henry knew, as did Owain, that in Roman law 'prince' denoted a sovereign ruler, which is why the latter's adoption of the title was viewed as a calculated act designed to proclaim both his distinctiveness and independence.

Owain was not so naïve as to think that his action would not attract the attention and criticism of the king, but he pressed on regardless because he believed that Henry's policies were not only a threat to his position and status, but they inhibited Gwynedd's expansion. Owain knew that Henry might make war on him but perhaps he felt that he had no choice but to persist in a struggle that might lead to defeat and humiliation. When war did come, in the summer of 1165, the forces arrayed against him must have filled him with dread, yet perhaps Owain thought that if he had no chance of winning an outright victory there might still be some advantage for him in spoiling operations: by delaying, harrying and the wearing down of Henry and his army. He at least had the satisfaction of leading a combined force of Welsh princely contingents, for it was with some pride that he mentioned 'the five armies of our side' in a subsequent letter to Louis VII.[5] Yet he knew that even this might not be enough to give him and his native allies a fighting chance against Henry's formidable army, and the

'Faithful and devoted friends': Owain and Louis VII

hired Hiberno-Scandinavian navy; hence his attempt to open diplomatic relations with the French king.

Who counselled or advised Owain to open negotiations with Louis is not known, nor do we know the extent or scale of his knowledge of wider European affairs. This is not to suggest that he was entirely ignorant of events or matters of importance on the continent, but simply that his focus had been on consolidating his power and maintaining the integrity of his kingdom in the face of a more powerful and aggressive neighbour. Besides trade and commercial contacts it is likely that Owain's knowledge of, and contact with, Europe came by way of the church. The agencies of the church were omnipresent and its influence was international, transcending state boundaries. If we accept F.W. Maitland's opinion that 'the medieval church was a state', then Wales was but a small part of it, but a part nonetheless, with links throughout Europe. That said, it is evident from Owain's communications with Louis that there had been little contact previously between Gwynedd and France due to 'the rarity of travellers coming and going and the distance of places [between us]'.[6] This is something Owain intended to put right because, as he wrote, 'from now on I shall endeavour diligently to obtain [Louis's friendship] by both writing and messenger'.[7]

By the autumn of 1164, if not earlier, Owain had become aware of Henry's difficulties in his other dominions and it was his intention to exploit them to the full. Owain may have been alerted to the fact that all was not rosy in the Angevin camp when a serious rift developed between the king and his archbishop, Thomas Becket. It is perhaps no mere coincidence that Owain's growing belligerence and initial embassy to the court of Louis VII was conducted during the period when, from the summer of 1163, Becket and Henry II became involved in an acrimonious quarrel over jurisdictional rights involving the church and state. Indeed, Owain may have witnessed the opening salvo of this feud which was fired first by Becket at the Council of Woodstock. Owain was no friend of Becket for the two were at odds mainly over the jurisdiction of the church in north Wales, but the Welshman was aware of the problems the archbishop might cause the king. They may not have been allies, but Becket and Owain shared a mutual desire to seek the aid of King Louis of France in their conflicts with King Henry of England.

For his part Louis, too, was seeking allies in his struggle with his Angevin vassal. Although Henry II was king of England, by virtue of his French possessions, he was Louis's vassal. In France Henry was noble rather than royal, he was duke of Normandy and Count of Anjou (along with a host of other similar titles), but Louis was king. Territorially Louis was the poor relation to the land-rich Henry but, constitutionally, he was his superior, his feudal overlord. The problem for Louis was not just in enforcing his authority, but in having Henry recognise it. As John Gillingham put it:

> Henry II emphatically recognised Louis VII as his lord, and did so in fulsome terms. This was part of his habitual style, a readiness to use obsequious words: a kind of deference that sometimes crossed the line between courtesy and hypocrisy.[8]

Henry's challenging behaviour towards Louis is something he would never have tolerated in others, which is perhaps why Owain did not trust him and was determined to cast

'Faithful and devoted friends': Owain and Louis VII

off his allegiance at the earliest opportunity and seek a new overlord.

It is known that Owain dispatched at least four diplomatic missions to the French court between the autumn of 1164 and the spring of 1166, of which three are recorded in writing. Unfortunately, none of Owain's three surviving letters to Louis can be precisely dated, though Huw Pryce has made a convincing case for placing them in a chronological order that seems to fit the events of the period. The first letter was intended as an introduction because Owain was 'largely unknown up to now' to Louis but that, henceforth, he asked 'with the greatest perseverance of prayers that you may deign from now on to consider me... amongst your faithful and devoted friends'.[9] Best estimates suggest that this initial communication was dispatched sometime in the autumn of 1164 after Owain and his nephew, The Lord Rhys, broke their faith with Henry II and, according to the Norman chronicler, Robert of Torigny, attacked 'neighbouring lands'.[10]

The second letter, which followed early in 1165 before Henry's abortive summer campaign, was addressed to Louis's chancellor, Hugh de Champfleury, bishop of Soissons. Unlike his previous letter, this one is rather more direct:

> I give thanks to God the Father, my venerable one, and to your discretion concerning that which you committed to writing in your letter to me through my messenger Moses, namely that if I should again send my messenger to the lord king of France, I should make him come through you, so that with your help his purpose might be accomplished more effectively.[11]

The content of this letter suggests that Owain's initial contact with Louis may not have been as successful as he had wished but that with Bishop Hugh's advice and support, he hoped for a more productive outcome in his dealings with the king. It is possible that Louis, a pious but hard-working king, was distracted by the weight of business and at the prospect of the birth of a long-awaited son and heir in August 1165. Another explanation, offered by Owain himself in a subsequent letter, is that Louis simply did not trust either the messenger or the veracity of the missives addressed to him: 'I sent him [Guiradus] before into your presence with my letters, which you did not believe were mine, so we are told'.[12] Whatever the true explanation, Louis seemed slow to respond to, let alone act on, the entreaties of the self-styled king of Wales.

The mediation offered by Bishop Hugh appears to have worked for by the third and, as far as is known, last of Owain's letters the relationship between the two monarchs had developed appreciatively. This letter was certainly composed after the summer campaign of 1165 when the weather and difficulties in supply, rather than anything the Welsh had done, had contributed to Henry's ignominious defeat atop the Berwyn Mountains. The content of Owain's letter suggests that written communication had become more established and had amounted to more than the three surviving missives:

> For as often as I have informed you about myself and my cares by the writing of letters, you have received not only the letters but their bearers benevolently and treated them kindly.[13]

'Faithful and devoted friends': Owain and Louis VII

As he wrote this letter, Owain was clearly under pressure because 'difficulties are all around me at present'.[14] As he related the events of Henry's summer campaign to Louis, he was fearful that his luck would not hold and that another more devastating attack would be launched upon him and his allies:

> I do not wish my kind adviser [Louis] to be ignorant of the situation. Preceeded by no evil deeds of mine, in the past summer the king of England has waged against me the war which, as is known to you, he has planned for many days with the harshness of his tyranny. But when in the conflict the five armies of our side came together, thanks be to God and you, more of his men fell than mine. Having seen this… he moved the army towards England, not through our merits, perhaps, but through… the saints' intercession to God; however he left me uncertain of the outcome to the end, because he arranged neither a peace nor a truce with us. Angered therefore because the result had not turned out as he had hoped, on his departure he ordered the foreigners and all whom he had gathered together to defeat us to come with him against us again after next Easter.[15]

The reference to another attack sometime after Easter 1166 is interesting, because it suggests that either Henry II had deliberately publicised his intention to campaign again in the hope that the Welsh might come to terms, or that Owain had gathered this intelligence through covert means. In a realistic appraisal of his position, Owain made plain his concern to Louis: 'I have no way of evading his snares unless you grant me advice and help'.[16] In consequence of this Owain proposed a military alliance:

> I vigorously entreat your clemency that you will inform me through the bearer of this present letter whether you are resolved to wage war against him, so that in that war I may both serve you by harming him according to your advice and take vengeance for the war he waged against me.[17]

Owain was a realist and he knew that military might was not the only weapon available to Henry II. Economically, Wales was almost entirely dependent on England, a fact noted by Gerald of Wales who advised any would-be conqueror of the Welsh that

> ... he must make every effort to stop the Welsh buying the stocks of cloth, salt and corn which they usually import from England. Ships manned with picked troops must patrol the coast, to make sure that these goods are not brought by water across the Irish Sea or the Severn Sea...[18]

The principles of an economic blockade, by land and sea, had the potential to be effective against a nation that did not possess anything approaching a navy. The Welsh had, for some time, been dependent on ships supplied by Hiberno-Scandinavian communities in Ireland which is perhaps why, for the first time, Henry employed them, partly to aid his campaign but also to deny their use to Owain. Gerald also had some timely advice on how to proceed in a military conquest of the Welsh:

> Any prince who is really determined to conquer the Welsh and to govern them in peace... should first of all understand that for a whole year at least he must devote his every effort and give his undivided attention to the task which he has undertaken. He can never hope to conquer in one single battle a people which will never draw up its forces to engage an enemy in the field,

'Faithful and devoted friends': Owain and Louis VII

and will never allow itself to be besieged inside fortified strongpoints. He can beat them only by patient and unremitting pressure applied over a long period.[19]

Fortunately for Owain, Henry was never able to focus fully on Wales and channel his considerable resources into its military subjection. Distracted by his continental commitments, Henry was drawn away to face what was developing into a strengthening coalition of enemy forces ranged against him. That Henry II was aware of the gathering storm is indicated by Arnulf, bishop of Lisieux, one of his councillors, who wrote to Becket outlining the pressure being brought to bear on his master. According to Bishop Arnulf, a man who was later to fall foul of the king and be unjustly hounded out of office, Henry was beset on all sides by the French, Flemish, Bretons, Poitevins, Gascons, Scots and, of course, the Welsh. Yet the one-time royal councillor and justiciar of Normandy was sure that Henry would prevail because 'He is a great, indeed the greatest of monarchs, for he has no superior of whom he stands in awe, nor subject who may resist him'.[20]

In the event, Owain did not need to resist Henry, nor did he need the aid of the French king he had courted so assiduously for so long, for the spring campaign never materialised. Henry left for the continent in March 1166 to deal with the rebellious Bretons and he did not return for another four years. As Henry was crushing the Bretons, trouble was brewing in Aquitaine, and worse was to come in 1167 when he found himself at war with his overlord King Louis of France. Whereas, once news of Henry's armies on the march filled him with dread, Owain was filled with delight as he heard of the king's mounting difficulties abroad.

Thus Owain was free to exploit the king's absence and press ahead with the expansion of Gwynedd and the consolidaton of his power both within his own kingdom and in Wales as a whole. The two were never to lock horns again for when Henry did return to England, Owain was dead and the fate of Gwynedd lay in the hands of his quarrelsome sons.

In seeking to establish independent political relations with the French king, Owain evidently saw the possibility of bringing pressure to bear on Henry II from other quarters and the means whereby he might renounce his oaths of fealty and homage. Whether Owain intended to submit himself to Louis's 'conveniently distant' overlordship is another matter, and there are doubts inasmuch as his request to become one of the French king's 'faithful men and friends' is somewhat vague and technically ambiguous, but it was a pretext sufficient for him to reject Henry's overlordship.[21] By 1168 relations between Louis and his Welsh 'vassals' had quickened and broadened to include not just Owain but, in the words of a contemporary, John of Salisbury, 'the other kings of Wales' who included, presumably, Rhys ap Gruffudd of Deheubarth and the 'five… greater men of Wales' referred to by Ralph of Diceto as having attended Woodstock.[22] According to Salisbury, the Welsh rulers dispatched an embassy to the French court which 'promised aid to the French king and offered him hostages' after which it 'departed under an obligation' whose precise meaning and details were never spelt out.[23] It is interesting to speculate on whether Owain was fully cognizant of the wider implications of his becoming a vassal of the French Crown to whom Henry also owed allegiance in respect of his French territories. His kingship of England notwithstanding, Henry might have found himself on a par with one from whom he was attempting to wrest a more formal recognition of his superior status; the potential for the disruption of traditional bonds of allegiance and notional ties of overlordship was infinite.

In the event, the Welsh were never obliged to test their new-found friendship with the Capetian king of France; circumstances quickly conspired to abort further contact between them. Indeed, it may reasonably be argued that the basis of their good relations was little more than words and gestures. Whatever the truth of the matter, the conclusion of peace between Louis VII and Henry II at Montmirail in January 1169, followed by Owain Gwynedd's death in November 1170, served to sabotage their fledgling diplomatic and political relationship. By 1174 it was irrevocably severed by the decision of Rhys ap Gruffudd to aid his erstwhile foe Henry II rather than his late ally Louis VII when the armed struggle between Capetian and Angevin was resumed.

VII

'Equity, prudence and princely moderation': Politics, Power and Princely Rule

> I want to stress to you with what equity, prudence and princely moderation three rulers have governed the three parts of Wales in our times: in Gwynedd Owain Gwynedd, son of Gruffudd ap Cynan; in Deheubarth Maredudd ap Gruffudd, Owain's nephew, who died young; and in Powys Owain Cyfeiliog.[1]

OWAIN AP GRUFFUDD AP Cynan had clearly impressed Gerald of Wales a wordly-wise and well-travelled man for whom flattery was reserved only for those who deserved it. That Gerald felt compelled to praise the wise rule of a man he considered to be morally repugnant for marrying his first cousin strongly suggests that Owain was indeed someone possessed of exceptional qualities. That Owain is praised alongside a nephew and son-in-law, rulers of the other two 'great' native powers, Deheubarth and Powys, indicates the extent of his familial influence on the ruling

'Equity, prudence and princely moderation'

families of Wales. Writing some 20 years after Owain's death, Gerald was reflecting on the greatness of a man whose pre-eminence was a widely acknowledged fact in native Wales in the last decade of his life.

That Owain ruled is not in doubt, but whether he 'governed' in the sense implied by Gerald of Wales is a matter for debate. Gerald's knowledge and experience of government were based primarily on the more developed Angevin model presided over by Henry II and his successors, Richard I and John. Arguably, the most significant developments of Henry II's reign were in revenue raising and law making, both of which were underpinned by careful record keeping. Henry has long been credited with being the founder of the English legal system but in the opinion of M.T. Clanchy:

> …more was probably due to the effects of writing as a technology than to Henry himself or any other individual. The impressive legal monument left by Henry II was the product of fossilization rather than a deliberate policy… Writing proved to be a more powerful and intractable force than anyone had bargained for.[2]

Unlike in England or in France under Louis VII, the evidence for royal administration, its organisation and operation in the Welsh kingdoms is scarce, so we are forced to rely on supposition and speculation. Government is a term with lofty pretensions which almost presupposes the existence of a state with a functioning bureaucracy. Although both had developed sufficiently by the thirteenth century, in concept and design, to serve the needs of the rulers of Gwynedd, 'state' and 'bureaucracy', like 'government', are terms hardly to be applied without qualification before that date, especially when lordship and rulership will do.

It is as lords of men that we first encounter Gruffudd ap Cynan and his son Owain Gwynedd, and the chief attributes of lordship – leadership and dependence – manifest themselves most clearly in war. Kings in name but warlords by nature, they roamed the land almost at will with their noble companions, plundering and 'ravaging' as they went. They did this in the name of honour and in the cause of glory and, as befitting a 'heroic' warrior society, in search of reputation. They were essentially conquerors of men rather than of territory, which is why it was a neighbour's moveable wealth rather than the territory itself, that seems to have interested them. Thus did the native chroniclers celebrate Owain's and Cadwaladr's return from their campaign to Ceredigion in 1136

> happily rejoicing... after honourably obtaining the victory and after obtaining an exceeding number of captives and spoils and costly rainment and armour.[3]

Laden with spoil, these royal warlords would return home and reward their faithful followers, and in so doing establish the means of controlling them. These dependents became the king's key supporters, a ruling noble elite bound to a common overlord by ties of service and comradeship in arms. Whether this can be accepted as evidence for what David Moore believes to be 'the existence of a form of feudalism', and, if linked to the bestowal of land, be 'interpreted as a form of feudal tenure', are moot points.[4] Sir J.E. Lloyd thought so, for he cites an early example of what he interpreted to be a form of feudal tenure:

'Equity, prudence and princely moderation'

'Uchtryd became Cadwgan's vassal, receiving from him Meirionydd and Cyfeiliog on the purely feudal condition, of which this is the first example in Welsh history, that he would be faithful to his lord and render him succour against all enemies'.[5]

It was primarily by means of military lordship, as distinct from purely landlordship and economic lordship, that they ruled so that terror more than territory formed the basis of their authority. This is not to underestimate the importance of the latter for the holding or ownership of land contributed to defining the status and importance of a man, but it is probably true to say that the territorial kingdom, as opposed to the rule of peoples, was an evolving concept.

The stages in that evolution from warlords to landlords, from governors to administrators, is touched upon by Wendy Davies, who states that whereas Gruffudd ap Llywelyn 'spent most of his reign campaigning' so that 'he had little time for "rule" in any real sense of the word', Gruffudd ap Cynan was determined to govern.[6] The *Historia* suggests that Gruffudd not only had some rule-making power but that the kingdom had developed an embryonic state apparatus supported by an administrative machine capable of collecting taxes, levying military service and enforcing the law. The division of the kingdom into *cantrefi* with further subdivisions into commotes or *cymydau*, each with its own *llys* to act as the focal point for royal authority, is suggestive of developing statehood. That the majority of these territorial divisions were well established by the early twelfth century is attested to by an unnamed poet who described Wales as a land of many districts each 'shaped by geography, history, and sentiment, and one which contemporaries recognized and with which they could identify'.[7] Therefore the administrative framework so familiar to us today of *gwlad*, *cantref* and *cwmwd*, was becoming more clearly defined and their bureaucraticisation more carefully developed. Gradually, over time, the kings of Wales evolved from being simply 'tribal' chiefs of men to becoming rulers of territorial states. Arguably, it was during the course of the twelfth century, nearly three quarters of which was dominated by the rule of Gruffudd ap Cynan and his son Owain Gwynedd, that witnessed this transformation whereby kingships evolved into kingdoms.

Owain's consolidation and defence of his authority in his dominions rested upon his mastery of the art of warfare, and this in turn rested upon his ability to turn his capital resources into available wealth. His subjects were expected to render dues and services that included time-honoured obligations by the freemen to provide accomodation for the king's officers when touring the *llysoedd*, and by the bondmen to provide for the upkeep of their lord's warhorse. Where previously the ruler's authority had been spasmodic in its impact and often nominal in character, the territorial division of the kingdom provided him with the framework and the means to better and more effectively govern his domain. If, as is generally believed, the primary function of medieval government was the maintenance of order and the collection of revenue, then Owain may be credited with fulfilling this.

Increasingly, native rulers were coming to be judged as politicians, diplomats, justices and administrators; hence the praise heaped on Gruffudd ap Cynan by his biographer for having

'Equity, prudence and princely moderation'

... governed for many years successfully and powerfully with moderation and peace, and enjoyed neighbourly relations in accord with the kings nearest to him, namely Henry king of England, Murchadh king of Ireland, and the king of the Islands of Denmark.[8]

It may be significant that the *Historia* was composed during the reign of Gruffudd's son and successor, Owain, a period that witnessed further developments in the trappings of state. That Owain had a secretariat or at least the means, and the personnel, to draw up diplomatic documents, charters and letters, such as those sent to Thomas Becket and Louis VII, betrays a level of bureaucratic sophistication. Certainly, a subtle shift in thinking and emphasis on the part of the chroniclers can be detected. The author of the *Brut* could not resist remembering Gruffudd ap Cynan at his death in 1137 as a 'king and chief and leader and defender' whose worth was measured by the 'innumerable spoils and victories in wars', and weight in 'gold and silver and costly rainment' taken from his enemies.[9] Whereas it is predominantly as a warrior that Gruffudd is commemorated, his successor, Owain, was remembered 33 years later as 'a man of great renown and of infinite prudence and nobility' who 'had governed his countrey well and worthely 32 yeres', with only a passing reference to his 'victories beyond number'.[10]

Nevertheless, it must not be thought that taking on the mantle of civilian government in any way diminished Owain's accustomed role as a military leader. For, irrespective of the developing political and bureaucratic sophistication of Gwynedd, the exercise of real power never moved far beyond his ability to field an effective fighting force and to fund the construction of castles. At the heart of this 'fighting force', the core element that made it effective and the hub around which Welsh military life revolved, was the *teulu*: a body of well-trained professional troops pledged to protect their king. The royal retinue was an ever-present fact which served to remind the ruler that war was in large part his *raison d'etre*. Not that Owain alone maintained a *teulu*, a permanent military retinue, for others too within the *membra regis* or royal family, such as his sons, Cynan, Dafydd and Hywel and his brother, Cadwaladr, had *teuluoedd* of their own. Nevertheless, it was the *penteulu* of the king that took precedence at court, as it was his men who defended the royal *llys* when their master was in residence.

Yet if war enabled a ruler to 'lord it' over his neighbours, demonstrate his military prowess and enhance his reputation, it contributed little to the effective government of his own realm. War was an expensive business whose spiralling costs threatened to outstrip the resources of the native princes. As the raids of the eleventh century gradually gave way to the campaigns of the twelfth, rulers like Owain had to find the means to raise, fund and equip an army rather than a retinue. Owain's *teulu* was likely sufficient to meet the needs of a raid, but for a campaign he would need to draw on wider resources of manpower to fill the ranks of his *llu* or army. In one such campaign, to Ceredigion in 1136, Owain and Cadwaladr were said to have led

> a numerous force of picked warriors, about six thousand fine foot-soldiers and two thousand mailed horsemen most brave and ready for battle.[11]

It is likely that the 'mailed horsemen' or knights consisted of the combined *teuluoedd* of Owain, his sons, brother and

'Equity, prudence and princely moderation'

those of his four 'princely' allies supported by the *llu* of lower-rank foot soldiers. If we accept the numbers quoted by the chroniclers, this was an impressive show of force and the fact that Owain could field an army of 8,000 men suggests a level of organisation and administration consistent with primitive bureaucratic processes. Sean Davies has speculated that the

> ...muster of a great leader involved many individual units which would eventually gather under his sole command, but at its most local level the commote seems likely to have been the essential unit.[12]

It was no mean feat to be able to arm, train, clothe, feed and shelter so many men for prolonged service in the field. Indeed, beyond the sheer exhilaration of taking part in the fight, there was a more pressing purpose to Owain's military adventures, namely to secure the kingdom and enforce his will.

A large army notwithstanding, it was in the competitive area of new technology linked to castle building that Owain had to develop if he was to succeed in enforcing his will. The erection of a castle was a tangible expression of the consolidation of a ruler's power. It is clear from contemporary evidence that possession of a castle brought with it control of the lordship in which it was situated: when 'Hywel ab Owain sought Cadwaladr's portion of Ceredigion' he could not take possession of it until the 'castle at Aberystwyth was burnt'.[13] That he was adept at besieging, capturing and destroying castles is amply testified by the chroniclers who record the names of no fewer than a dozen castles that fell, some more than once, to Owain. In stark contrast we know little about Owain's castle building let alone any strategy linked to their location. The single exception is Tomen y Rhodwydd, 'probably the finest Welsh earthwork castle' according to Richard Avent, which was built by Owain in 1149 as part of a strategic plan to hold a newly-won territory and to defend the borders of Gwynedd.[14] Ironically, his brother Cadwaladr is credited with building two castles, at Llanrhystud and Cynfael near Tywyn. Although difficult to prove without archaeological investigation, it may be possible to assign a further half-dozen castles within Gwynedd to Owain.[15] In seeking a permanent and visible symbol of his authority by means of a network of earth and timber castles, Owain would require not just new sources of funding but the administration to effect their construction, maintenance and garrison.

The castle alone did not represent Owain's power; he could rely on a network of courts or *llysoedd*. Their purpose was to promote and consolidate Owain's authority by acting as the focal point or *caput* of their respective lordships. Here his subjects would render their submissions, perform their services and pay their dues. Although royal incomes may still have been mainly in kind, there can be little doubt that by the mid-twelfth century elements of a moneyed economy had penetrated deep into Welsh society. It is instructive that when 'his time to go from this world was approaching', it is in terms of coin rather than kind that Gruffudd ap Cynan 'divided all his wealth'.[16] According to his biographer, he willed between ten and twenty 'pieces of silver' to each of more than a dozen churches and monasteries in Wales, England and Ireland. These courts contributed to the maintenance of Owain's power, both real and symbolic, and provided the kingdom with the cohesion necessary for its consolidation.

The chief court, the hub around which royal governance revolved, was at Aberffraw on Anglesey, and, according to Gerald of Wales was, by history and tradition, 'one of the three royal palaces of Wales'.[17] Here business would be transacted, politics conducted and decisions made. Here also would be found the ruler's household staffed by his domestic servants, military retainers, courtiers and clerics, some of whom served as one of the 24 officers of the court. Largely domestic in origin and function, the elaborate hierarchy of court officials depicted in the lawbooks was somewhat out of step with the reality of developments in the latter half of the twelfth century. By this time the more significant of the court officers in Gwynedd, namely, the steward or *distain*, the chamberlain or *gwas ystafell*, possibly the court judge or *ynad llys*, and perhaps even the household priest or *offeiriad teulu*, had evolved sufficiently to be able to take a more active role in government which had itself become a more complex administrative operation.

There was little in the way of administrative specialisation and bureaucratic institutions, but that there were powerful forces at work making for change cannot be doubted. The catalysts for change were the rulers themselves since it was largely as a result of their ambition, drive and energy, for power, wealth and territory, which stimulated those around them into seeking new ways to best serve them. Consciously, and sometimes unconsciously, rulers and their 'leading men' imitated, copied and borrowed from their neighbours, the Crown and the Anglo-Norman Marcher Lords, so that theirs was a 'bureaucratic' hybrid composed of several layers extending from the centre almost web-like into the localities. Of course, to contemporaries, government must have seemed almost entirely a local affair and so it was and largely remained so, but as in England there was a discernible shift towards concentrating the business of government in the hands of those at the centre. Where that centre was depended very much on the whereabouts of the ruler around whom government was fashioned and in whom power was concentrated. As befitted the personal nature of Owain's rule, it was at Aberffraw, and at other important royal palaces such as Aber near Bangor, that he likely met his subjects as he went on progress through his lands. The importance of this aspect of royal rule is underlined by the fact that having recovered Gwynedd from his enemies, Gruffudd ap Cynan's biographer reports that he was encouraged 'to go on circuit around his patrimony' so that he might 'subdue Anglesey and Arfon and Llŷn and the cantrefs bordering England' by taking 'homage (*gwrogaeth*) from their people' (*gwerin*).[18]

Having inherited this system from his father, it is not unreasonable to suggest that Owain followed this example of itinerant lordship. Indeed, so far as the kingdom can be said to have had any unity, it rested solely in Owain's peripatetic court and household. The territories to which Owain acquired title by birth and inheritance – Gwynedd Uwch Conwy and part of Gwynedd Is Conwy – can be regarded as his personal patrimony to which were added during the course of his reign additional territories such as Meirionydd, Iâl, Tegeingl and, until lost in 1153, Ceredigion. These peripheral or border territories may have formed a loose confederation linked by dynastic ties and presumably some form of oath taking.

'Equity, prudence and princely moderation'

If neither the will nor consent of the people at large was considered a prerequisite for realising the potential of 'good lordship', it was essential that Owain have the willing consent of his 'leading men'. A descriptive term that recurs regularly in contemporary texts, the importance of these 'leading men' is such that they probably had a significant impact on Owain's rule and in the development of government and administration. These were the men with whom Owain hunted and generally consorted, in whom he trusted, of whom in war he boasted and on whom he relied for counsel. That their counsel was heeded is much in evidence in the native chronicles which offer tantalising glimpses of their work and worth. For example, it was 'through the counsel of their leading men that they [Owain and Cadwaladr] were reconciled in 1144'.[19] Again, when Henry II threatened the invasion of Gwynedd in 1157 Owain responded by 'summoning to him his sons and his leading men'.[20] Who these men were is not generally known, other than that they were often no whit less noble or powerful than the rulers they served. Rarely are we permitted to put names to them much less tie them to a particular district or locality, but one such glimpse is afforded by Gruffudd ap Cynan's biographer:

> Then Gruffudd sent messengers to the men of Anglesey and Arfon, and the three sons of Merwydd of Llŷn, Asser, Meirion and Gwgon, and other leading men to ask them to come in haste, talk to him. And without delay they came and greeted him, and told him, 'your coming is welcome'. Then he besought them with all his might to help him to obtain his patrimony, because he was their rightful lord.[21]

Nevertheless, it is equally clear that, ultimately, power rested in the ruler and though his counsellors could advise, forcefully at times, they might not be permitted to decide or dictate policy. At what point counsellors became councillors is not easy to determine, but that they did so by the thirteenth century is indicative of the gradual institutionalisation of significant aspects of royal government and administration. Although it is not until the early years of the thirteenth century that we have anything like a reliable reference to what appears to have been a properly constituted royal council, it is reasonable to assume that there had existed a council of sorts for some time before this. It was the personality and will of the ruler that dominated Gwynedd, and what mattered was not so much Owain's 'right' or 'power' to act independently of his 'leading men' but the way in which he exercised those rights and implemented his powers. In short, the sucessful ruler was the one who tempered his masterfulness with concessions.

The twelfth century witnessed a great increase in the nature and scope of administrative activity and no more so than in the law. Although the main body of native law was based on custom rather than on royal legislation, by the latter half of the twelfth century, if not earlier, Welsh kings had, for want of a better term, 'acquired' the power not only to 'amend', 'correct', 'amplify' and 'abbreviate' the laws but to 'grant' and 'abolish' them also. Nor can we rule out entirely the possibility, as expressed by Huw Pryce, 'that custom had itself been shaped in part by princely legislation, which may also have left its mark on some of the legal rules'.[22] Even the surviving texts of the Welsh laws, written by lawyers for lawyers and without acknowledging the patronage of

'Equity, prudence and princely moderation'

any one ruler, save Hywel Dda, betray their debt to the reforming zeal of rulers like Owain Gwynedd. Their arrogation of legislative power in matters of law and justice notwithstanding, kings may not have been entirely free to act, or thought it imprudent to do so, without consulting their nobility, particularly, but perhaps not exclusively, those in council.

Clearly, the ruler needed the advice and support of his nobility and, where appropriate, he shared his lordship with them, but the successful ruler was the one who managed at the same time to maintain his authority over them. Owain was among the more astute and sensitive rulers who realised that to behave with reckless abandon was to invite trouble and that it was in his interests to observe and respect the long-held customs of his subjects. Nevertheless, it was equally apparent that in order to meet the challenges of a changing world, Owain had to adapt and adopt, and often tested to the limit the tolerance of his subjects. The law, both native and borrowings from Angevin and later 'English' law, was taken in hand and fashioned according to the needs of rulers like Owain, thereby becoming an indispensible tool of government. Not that there was much to chose between governing and law-keeping since, in truth, they were not separate activities, which explains why the courts and councils of Welsh kings, in common with those on the continent, had always exhibited a strong judicial aspect. By the making, amending and enforcing of law and the dispensing of justice, native rulers were not only enhancing their status and prestige, but adding materially to their wealth and power. Gradually, but noticeably, the agencies of royal authority – the commotal courts and royal officers – assumed a greater role in the dispensing of justice which, in turn, contributed to the growth of the concept of the state and of public order within it.

Historians make much of the fluid nature of royal administration and the embryonic state of kingly bureaucracy in the late twelfth century. True there is a great deal that we do not know and, in an effort to understand the nature of native government, historians have turned, rightly, to compare the Welsh model with that found in England, but even this has its pitfalls. It assumes that the English model was anything but fluid and embryonic when, in fact, it too was experiencing changes every bit as fundamental as those to be found in the courts of Welsh rulers. According to Marjorie Chibnall, part of the difficulty in describing the changes in the English administration 'arises from the lack of a technical vocabulary, inevitable in a time of growth and change, when new institutions were only half formed and imperfectly defined'.[23] According to Rees Davies, 'None of the courts of the native Welsh rulers developed the specialisation of function which was coming to characterise the *curia regis* in England'.[24] It may be clear, as David Stephenson believes, 'that the majority of the officials associated with the central *curia* were employed in any business for which their talents made them suitable, without any clear differentiation of function'.[25] Preferring instead to err on the side of caution, the general consensus of opinion favours the existence of a loosely-organised secretariat staffed by a number of clerks, likely clerical, any one of whom was capable of drawing up and issuing Owain's acts and letters.

Whoever was responsible for drawing up the letters for Owain, it was clear that government was coming to rely increasingly on the written word. It was by means of the written word, in his letters to Archbishop Thomas Becket, King Louis of France, Bishop Hugh of Soissons and, more controversially, Bishop Bernard of St David's, that Owain expressed his power, status and ambitions.[26] According to Huw Pryce, 'The clerks who drafted letters for the rulers of Gwynedd generally conformed to western European epistolary conventions of the period' and although the five letters drawn up for Owain 'exhibit a varied pattern' they compare favourably with anything produced for Henry II and Louis VII.[27] Owain's communications reveal a subtle shift in title and emphasis that offer a revealing insight into his conception of his power. For much of his reign Owain styled himself as king or *rex* but this changed after 1165 when he adopted the title of prince or *princeps*. At no point did he style himself as king or prince of Gwynedd or north Wales, but rather he broadened the concept of his power and authority by embracing the whole of Wales. As early as 1140, only three years into his reign as ruler of Gwynedd, he styled himself as *rex Walliae* or king of Wales.[28] Nor did this change, for when we next encounter him in 'print', mainly during 1165, he is variously King Owain, Owain king of Wales or Owain king of the Welsh.[29]

However, there is some evidence to suggest that as early as 1163 Owain may have been experimenting with a new title, for in a letter to Pope Alexander III, Becket makes a mocking reference to 'the self-styled Prince Owain and the Welsh'.[30] From 1166 the ambiguity was set side and, henceforward, Owain adopted the title of prince though he did continue to vary the style by calling himself either prince of Wales (*Waliarum princeps*) or prince of the Welsh

(*Walensium princeps*). Both titles convey the elevated status and sense of national authority that Owain wished to arrogate to himself, the first as a territorial lord and the other as a leader of his people. Henry II's anger at Owain's use of this new title was shared by his archbishop, Thomas Becket, but after these two fell out, the latter had a change of heart. Doubtless motivated by personal as well as political reasons, Archbishop Becket embraced the change and, in three letters written between May and September 1169, he addressed Owain as prince of the Welsh.[31] It is possible that this change of title was the inspiration for, if not accompanied by, the adoption of a coronet or *talaith* and other trappings of royalty, such as a coronation ceremony and a seal with which to authenticate documents. Although not mentioned until 1240, the adoption of a coronet would have served to underline the significance and uniqueness of the title of prince. That Cadwaladr possessed a seal, which he used to authenticate his grant to Haughmond Abbey near Shrewsbury, strongly suggests that his brother Owain had one, though no evidence of its use has survived.[32]

Not content with becoming a prince of his people or opposing the will of a king, Owain, it seems, was determined to control, if not defy, the princes of the church. Native princely patronage represented a significant element in the church, a powerful institution that was second only to the coronet in terms of its authority, wealth and landholdings. Much of its wealth in land and privileges in law was as a result of munificent endowments and generous exemptions by Welsh kings. Its bishops and abbots, some of whom owed their clerical office to the patronage of native rulers, were among the wealthiest and most powerful men in the country and much the best educated. In return for their patronage, rulers like Owain Gwynedd expected their leading clerics to serve them as advisors and administrators, ambassadors and mediators; the evidence suggests that they did so willingly. In fact, some clerics acted as diplomatic messengers, men like Moses and Guiardus, who carried Owain's letters to the French king, Louis VII, in Paris. We know little about these men, other than that Moses may have been the brother of Meurig, bishop of Bangor, while Guiardus, in spite of his French name, was a Welshman whom Owain described as 'my private and familiar cleric and kinsman'.[33] These were men in whom Owain had complete trust; that was important because, as H. Hoffmann observed, 'the most important thing about a letter was the messenger'.[34] Both men not only carried important letters, they represented their royal master and they may even have been empowered to treat with King Louis and Bishop Hugh by speaking on behalf of Owain.

In peace and war the rulers' most enduring support came from the church which sustained the respective royal dynasties by informing and shaping lay opinion through sermons and ritual. Liturgical processions, royal ceremonial and, ultimately, its sanction of the exercise of secular authority by men consecrated to their positions, all contributed to enhancing the prestige of rulers like Owain. By publicly acknowledging them rulers *dei gratia*, by God's grace, the church also gave a focus to the participant aristocratic group whose own élite status was thus recognised and utilised. Increasingly the nobility were becoming more regularly employed alongside their clerical counterparts as agents and executants of royal authority. The Gwynedd of

Owain ap Gruffudd ap Cynan was in the vanguard of these changes. That Owain employed, and came to rely on the support and advice of, clerics is shown by his recruitment of Simon of Clynnog, archdeacon of Bangor. Described by his contemporaries as 'a man of great honour and dignity', Simon had served Owain's father faithfully for a number of years and was with him when he died.[35] Simon was likely among those whom the chroniclers described as Owain's 'leading men' for he was 'a man of great authority' to whom princes, both secular and clerical, turned for advice.[36] This is not to suggest that the relationship between prince and church was without problems, since there were tensions and pressures here too. The church dominated much of the public life, politics and culture of Wales. Naturally, the princes sought to control the church and they attempted to do so through a combination of patronage and coercion, depending on the pliancy of the personnel or institutions involved.

Therefore, if Owain can be said to have had a church policy it focused almost exclusively on its control and independence. As the diocesan model and its territorial authority established themselves and evolved in Wales during the eleventh and more certainly the twelfth century, the Welsh came to be represented by four bishops who held sway over Bangor, Llandaff, St Asaph and St David's. The boundaries of the diocese of Bangor were roughly coincident with those of the kingdom of Gwynedd so that here, at least, Owain's influence would count for a great deal. Unfortunately for him he got off to a shaky start when he failed his first big test in securing a pliant successor to another of his father's advisors, Bishop David of Bangor, who died sometime between late 1138 and early 1139. A

'Equity, prudence and princely moderation'

Welshman named Meurig succeeded to the see and was sponsored by the Anglo-Norman bishops of Hereford and Chichester who presented their clerical colleague to King Stephen at Worcester Cathedral in December 1139. Meurig was expected to swear fealty to the English king and submit to the authority of Theobald, Archbishop of Canterbury who would then conduct his consecration. However, as J.E. Lloyd put it, 'a hitch arose' when Meurig informed his hosts that 'he was not prepared to swear fealty to the king, having been forbidden to do so by a man for whom he had the profoundest veneration', namely, Simon of Clynnog.[37] It is likely that Simon's advice to Bishop Meurig was given with the full support, if not at the instigation, of Owain who wished to avoid any act of submission to either king or archbishop. According to J.E. Lloyd, Meurig was 'possessed of no great force of character and his scruples were soon overborne'.[38] As Conway Davies put it:

> The taking of the oath of fealty to the English crown, if fulfilled, would inevitably bring the bishop into controversy and conflict with the princes. The very taking of the oath of fealty was itself an infringement of their sovereignty.[39]

An angry Owain wrote to Bishop Bernard of St David's in an effort to elicit his support in ejecting Meurig whom he and his brother Cadwaladr claimed had 'entered the church of St Daniel like a thief, without any invitation from them'.[40] A meeting was proposed for 1 November 1140 at Aberdyfi where Owain and Cadwaladr hoped to discuss the matter with Bishop Bernard, along with Simon of Clynnog and Anarawd ap Gruffudd, ruler of Deheubarth. We do not know if the meeting took place but if it did, it failed in its bid to replace Meurig who, after some years in exile, entered his diocese and took up residence at the bishop's lodgings close to the cathedral. The relationship between Bishop Meurig and Owain Gwynedd remained frosty however, and sometime in the 1150s he was again exiled, never to return to his diocese.

As Owain extended the boundaries of his kingdom eastward towards Chester during the 1160s, the diocese of St Asaph also came within the orbit of his power. Created, or possibly re-created, in 1143 the diocese had been ministered by Gilbert, an Anglo-Norman bishop, who was no friend to Owain. Indeed, according to Glanmor Williams, Gilbert's

> ... appointment looks very much like a hastily devised expedient designed to safeguard the life of the church... from falling under the ecclesiastical influence of a would-be independent archbishop of St. David's and the political influence of the prince of Gwynedd.[41]

Undeterred by this blatant attempt by Archbishop Theobald to undermine native influence over the church in north-east Wales, when the opportunity presented itself Owain simply drove Bishop Gilbert into exile. Nor did his successor, Bishop Godfrey, fare any better. Consecrated in 1160, he was driven out of his diocese by Owain in 1166, never to return. Even when he was ordered to return to St Asaph by Thomas Becket in 1169, Godfrey, probably wisely, refused, preferring instead to live the life of an exile in the comfortable, and safer, surroundings of Abingdon Abbey in Oxfordshire. It would be another six years, in 1175, before he was forced to resign his Welsh bishopric.

Bishop Bernard's attempt to wrest control of the church in

'Equity, prudence and princely moderation'

Wales from the power of Canterbury by seeking to establish an independent archbishopric of St David's was supported by both Owain and Cadwaladr. The brothers knew that ecclesiastical subjugation was allied to, and underpinned by, English political control: they were indivisible. Of course, their objection was not to the principle of secular control of the church, just that it should not be in the hands of, or exercised by, an English king. Nor did they want bishops of Welsh dioceses, especially Bangor and St Asaph, making professions of obedience to an English archbishop. Owain was determined that the next time the see of Bangor became vacant he would ensure the appointment of a man acceptable to himself. That opportunity came in August 1161 when, after nearly 22 years in post, the exiled Meurig died. This time Owain was in a strong enough position to exert some influence over the appointment of a successor and he wrote to the exiled archbishop of Canterbury, Thomas Becket, requesting permission to have his nominee, Arthur of Bardsey, consecrated in Ireland. In his letter Owain makes plain that 'the obligation of undertaking the guardianship and care of that church belongs to us', and that Becket 'should grant our petition readily, since it is our will, and not any law, which compels us to submit ourselves to you'.[42] In short, Owain's appointee would offer his obedience to Canterbury as a favour rather than as a right.

If Owain hoped to exploit Becket's exile by pressurising him into agreeing the terms of the appointment, he was disappointed. Becket refused Owain's forceful request and insisted on having his own nominee appointed to the bishopric. The resulting stalemate left the see vacant, though there is reason to suspect that Owain went ahead and had

Arthur consecrated in Ireland. A vengeful Becket enlisted the support of the pope, Alexander III, in his increasingly bitter dispute with the prince of the Welsh. In their determination to bring Owain to heel, they tried to embarrass and undermine him by attacking his marriage to Cristin, the daughter of Gronw ab Owain ab Edwin. Cristin was Owain's second wife whom he married sometime during the 1140s, but because she was his first cousin and closely related in blood, their union was not permitted under canon law. Owain was outraged that a marriage transacted over 20 years ago was belatedly attracting the criticism of the papacy. He saw it for what it was: a cynical attempt by Becket to undermine his objection to Canterbury's disputed authority over the church in Wales and Gwynedd in particular. The fact that Archbishop Theobald, Becket's predecessor, had also tried, more than a decade earlier, to make political capital out of Owain's marriage served to harden the latter's resolve to defy his ecclesiastical opponents. In a letter to the exiled archbishop of Canterbury, Thomas Becket, dated February 1169, Pope Alexander expressed his anger and frustration at Owain's defiance:

> Know that we have been told that Owain, prince of Wales, has refused to receive the letter which we sent to him about his cousin, whom he is alleged to keep as his wife, and he has not sent that cousin away in accordance with our warning.[43]

It is clear from the letter that Owain had retained the allegiance of the clergy in Gwynedd who stood by him in defiance of the papacy, for the pope added, 'Equally, the archdeacon of Bangor has defied our letter, showing no desire to give it any kind of obedience'.[44]

'Equity, prudence and princely moderation'

This was particularly galling for Becket who had enlisted the support of Archdeacon David in his conflict with Owain. However, the archdeacon, who had previously sworn fealty to the archbishop, deserted his patron and offered his support to Owain. Whether this was done on grounds of conscience or due to pressure applied by Owain will never be known. Although hardly an impartial participant in the affair, Becket believed that the clergy of Bangor had been forced to comply with Owain's instructions, for in a letter to them sent in the summer of 1169, he said that:

> The Lord Pope has mercifully absolved you from the oath which Owain, prince of the Welsh, is said to have extorted from you in contravention of good custom and the teaching of the sacred canons.[45]

Becket broadened his conflict with Owain to include the archdeacon whom he accused of infidelity and of inheriting his ecclesiastical office rather than of being fairly appointed. Pope Alexander seemingly washed his hands of the whole affair when he empowered Becket to act as he saw fit:

> Since it belongs to your office to punish such audacity with ecclesiastical severity, especially since you know more about the matter than we do, we leave whatever you decide should be done to the judgement of your discretion. For we shall ratify and confirm whatever sentence you issue against them.[46]

Twice more Becket wrote to Owain in an attempt to induce his submission but he would not be moved. In one letter Becket wrote:

> We know that you are a wise man, who knows how to weigh good and evil, right from wrong, with the subtle measure of

reason, who thinks frequently of your death, for as experience teaches, young men die soon, and easily, and it is impossible for old men to live long... they fade away, and death, unseen creeps stealthily and slowly through every limb of the body and through every fading sense.[47]

Even in the face of a cynical attempt to manipulate the aging prince into compliance by playing upon his mortality and fear of death, Owain stood firm. At best Becket had underestimated his opponent but, at worst, he had misjudged him, for if Owain would not yield to reason he was unlikely to give in to threats. Even the intervention of Louis VII, who offered to mediate between the disputing parties, failed to resolve the impasse. No doubt frustrated at his lack of success and by Owain's stubborn refusal to yield, Becket eventually excommunicated him.

Owain died of natural causes on 23 November 1170 and, in spite of the sentence of excommunication pronounced upon him, he was honourably buried in Bangor Cathedral. Thomas Becket was murdered five weeks later, on 29 December, on the steps of the altar in Canterbury Cathedral. He too was buried with great solemnity not far from the place where he was murdered.

VIII

'Making a good end': Death and Reputation

> In the month of November, died Owain Gwynedd ap Gruffudd ap Cynan, a man of great renown and of infinite prudence and nobility, the bulwark and strength of Wales, unconquered from his youth, after victories beyond number, without having ever refused a man the request that was made to him.[1]

THE NATIVE CHRONICLERS DID not so much lament as laud Owain Gwynedd at his death. To them he was a leader worthy of praise and remembrance for he had frustrated those who were minded to 'annihilate all Welshmen' and had undermined those 'purposing to carry into bondage and to destroy all the Britons'.[2] In bardic encomia military leadership and courage on the battlefield take pride of place because Owain was, first and foremost, a warrior, a man who took as much delight in planning and preparing a raid or battle as participating in it. He was no backroom general; he led from the front risking life and limb alongside those with whom he lived, trained and commanded in combat. To judge from the native chronicles and bardic poetry

Owain was personally involved in at least a dozen raids and battles, almost all of which were successful. As Paul Barbier opined, 'If Gruffudd ap Cynan was the hero of Welsh defensive warfare, Owain was the hero of victory'.[3] He led and maintained a well-oiled military machine that had at its centre the *teulu*, his household troops, men on whom he relied and trusted with his life. Among those who served Owain were Gwalchmai ap Meilyr, a court poet and member of this warrior élite who gloried in his master's reputation, victories and generosity:

> I exalt a brave lion, a nature like lightning,
> I exalt the fairest of the princes of Britain.
>
> My father exalted the great king his father
> With a skilled muse, rich blessings were his;
> And I too will exalt a high leader of battle.
>
> He pours forth wealth and wealthy gifts.
>
> Out of his gains he gave me ungrudgingly
> Firm-fleshed horses, honourable grace,
> And he knew me as eager to fight in the forefront –
> His many blades, armed, champion wolf of the pack.[4]

It was by dint of his military efforts and by the sheer force of his personality that Owain maintained his hegemony in Gwynedd. His ruthless treatment of rivals, including family members, marked him out as a ruler of single-minded determination. By the end of his reign Owain had succeeded in imposing a degree of political and territorial unity in Gwynedd that established it as the leading kingdom in Wales.

'Making a good end': Death and Reputation

Indeed, the credit for establishing Gwynedd's primacy in Welsh affairs is due, primarily, to the work of two rulers, Gruffudd ap Cynan and his son Owain Gwynedd. They withstood the external pressures of Marcher ambition and royal intervention while repairing the dynastic fissures that regularly threatened to tear their territorial power apart. Between them, they created a stable and prosperous kingdom by strengthening their hold on church and state and by wisely, if only periodically, acknowledging English suzerainty. They were also responsible for originating and promoting the idea that a ruler of Gwynedd possessed authority over Wales as a whole, and, as if to emphasise the fact of their primacy, to Owain Gwynedd goes the credit of being the first of his countrymen to cultivate a diplomatic friendship with a foreign ruler. This shows a remarkable grasp on his part of the wider European stage. Father and son had reigned for over 70 years, a period that allowed for a continuity of effort and direction and for the cultivation of the arts, not just of war, but of peace also.

Owain was a multi-dimensional character, a man trained for war but possessed of the skills and instincts of a diplomat and peacemaker. He was, in the words of Archbishop Thomas Becket, 'a wise man, who knows how to weigh good and evil, right and wrong, with the subtle measure of reason'.[5] These qualities were very much in evidence in the summer of 1165 for in a story related by Gerald of Wales, Owain, locked in bitter conflict with Henry II, ably demonstrated why he was acquiring a reputation for wisdom, 'equity, prudence and princely moderation'.[6]

The leaders of the English army had burnt down certain Welsh churches, with their villages and churchyards. As a result the sons of Owain Gwynedd, supported by a band of young soldiers who were with them, bitterly harangued their father, and fellow princes, too, swearing that they would never in future spare any English churches. Everyone present was on the point of agreeing to this, but Owain, who was well known among his peers for his great wisdom and moderation, quelled the tumult. "I do not agree with you at all," he said. "On the contrary, we ought to be pleased with what has happened and rejoice. Unless we have God on our side, we are no match for the English. By what they have done they have alienated Him. He can avenge Himself and us, too, in the most striking way. Let us accordingly promise God devoutly that from this moment on we will pay greater reverence and honour than ever before to all churches and holy places."[7]

As far as is known, Gerald of Wales never met Owain Gwynedd and nor was he present when the latter allegedly uttered the words attributed to him. It may be apocryphal but why Gerald should manufacture a lie to enhance the reputation of a man who died an excommunicate is beyond comprehension. In fact, there is no compelling reason to doubt the tenor of what has been attributed to Owain, presumably by those present and in his hearing, men such as the Lord Rhys and Owain Cyfeiliog, both of whom were well known to Gerald. It is, perhaps, the closest we are likely to get to Owain speaking to us in his own words for although we have his letters, it is difficult to disentangle his personality from the official verbiage of his clerks. Gerald's story fits our conception of Owain as a man of courage and conviction, remaining calm, keeping his head as those around him lost

'Making a good end': Death and Reputation

theirs, as he and his allies awaited the expected onslaught of Henry's formidable army.

This is reflected in the subtle but discernible shift in the attitude of the native *literati* towards their rulers who came to be regarded not so much as all-conquering war leaders, important though this was, but as protectors, peacemakers and law-enforcers. The ruler, be he king or prince, stood at the heart of developments in war, politics, government and administration; each of these was conducted in his name and each was effected by means of his authority. The successful rulers were those able to convert this authority into power and, among the first of them to do this successfully, to an appreciable degree, was the twelfth-century ruler of Gwynedd, Owain ap Gruffudd ap Cynan. Hitherto the increase of a ruler's power had seemed tied to the expansion of his authority, usually and primarily by military means, but territorial expansion has its limits and can be dangerous if it outruns the means of control by contemporary modes of administration. After spending some 30 years in an almost unremitting struggle to expand, defend and ultimately, to consolidate the hard-won territories that made up his domain, Owain may have reached that limit by 1167.

Having scored a military and, in seeking the aid of Louis VII, diplomatic triumph over his erstwhile foe King Henry II of England in 1165, Owain could turn to increasing the range and scope of his authority within his own domain. Although the way in which he achieved this is largely speculation, it is possible to suggest that he did so by reconstructing the pattern of his authority within his dominions and by initiating a thorough reorganisation of his lands. The gradual institutionalisation and territorialisation of Owain's authority were vitally important if he was to secure the future of his dynasty. Indeed, it may be argued that a ruler's greatest achievement was not that he might create a large dominion, but that he introduced to it the art of government. Owain became the instrument of law, order, security and prosperity. He offered his subjects protection, justice and political unity in return for their obedience, loyalty, personal service and their conscription in war, which was no less invaluable than their support in peace. Owain was master in his own kingdom and little occurred without his approval or consent. Gerald of Wales may have had Owain in mind when he wrote that 'rumour does in truth fly on wings to kings and princes, from whom scarce anything may be hid, notable events are ever quick to reach them'.[8] Owain's lordship or *tywysogiaeth* was limited only by his own energy, ambition and resources, and, of course, by what his subjects and English kings were prepared to tolerate.

> After taking penance and holy confession and repentance and the communion of the virtues of the Body of Christ and extreme unction his soul departed to the mercy of God.[9]

Owain died on 23 November 1170 and was buried in Bangor Cathedral, his tomb taking pride of place in the wall of the presbytery close to the altar. The high regard in which Owain was held was very much in evidence in the years after his death, for his tomb became something of an attraction with visitors. This suggests that the tomb was an elaborate affair that may have sported either an effigy or some such carving topped quite possibly by a canopy.[10] Among the more distinguished visitors were Gerald of

'Making a good end': Death and Reputation

Wales and Baldwin, archbishop of Canterbury, who were invited to the cathedral to be 'shown the tombs of Owain Gwynedd and his brother Cadwaladr, who were buried in a double vault in the cathedral by the high altar'.[11] Owain died under sentence of excommunication pronounced upon him by 'the blessed martyr Thomas [Becket]… because he had committed public incest with his first cousin' so that he was considered unfit for a proper Christian burial.[12] Baldwin, who was in Bangor as part of his tour of Wales preaching and recruiting for the crusade in 1188, ordered Gwion, the bishop of Bangor 'to watch for an opportunity of removing his body from the cathedral and to do this as quickly as possible'.[13] The opportunity never arose since those with the power to disinter him were minded not to do so because in life he had been a generous patron and in death an icon embodying all the virtues of a Welsh hero.

So far as the political future was concerned, Owain's intentions are never clear to us, the passage of time has seen to that, but it seems that as far as his contemporaries were concerned, his eldest son, Hywel, was the designated heir. It is inconceivable that a man as astute as Owain would not have put measures in place to ensure a smooth succession and to preserve a lifetime's hard work. His attempt to secure the integrity of the kingdom for his heir-designate called for a fundamental re-thinking of the nature and status of his patrimony, and of himself as its ruler. In styling himself prince of Wales and prince of the Welsh, Owain was providing a clear affirmation of his right to rule beyond the borders of his patrimony in Gwynedd. The adoption of the title and style of prince was a prescient piece of politicking by Owain that did not mean a diminution of his status and power but rather the opposite, for as J. Beverley Smith has said, he 'did not cease to be king of Gwynedd in order to be prince of Gwynedd, ... he chose to present himself as prince of the Welsh (*princeps Wallensium*)'.[14]

Owain further legitimised his position, and that of his principality, by insisting on his claim to be recognised as the heir and successor not just of Gruffudd ap Cynan but also of Rhodri Mawr. This continuity of succession claimed a much sought-after antiquity, which could be used to uphold his right within Gwynedd, to set aside indigenous native lordship in *cantref* or commote in favour of treating these lands as administrative districts and their lords as his provincial governors. Alternatively, he placed members of his own family in these districts, such as in Meirionydd where his brother, Cadwaladr, and later his son, Cynan, were installed as his viceroys. This was by no means easy, for status and kinship were no less important to a ruler of a single *cantref* or commote as to a ruler of many, so that the interests of the kindred rather than any one man were being set aside by Owain. With these measures in place, allied to a strong, unified and well-governed realm, Owain's successor should have been able to build upon solid foundations and flourish, but that was not to be. Within months of Owain's death, the kingdom had descended into chaos and civil war, and at the Battle of Pentraeth on Anglesey, Dafydd ab Owain killed Hywel, his half-brother. For the best part of the next three decades, Gwynedd suffered intermittent conflict and political instability until the accession of Llywelyn Fawr. Despite his failure to secure Gwynedd for his heir-designate, Owain's attempt did at least provide a model for his successors, most notably his grandson Llywelyn the Great.

'Making a good end': Death and Reputation

What of Owain Gwynedd? What kind of man was he? It is almost impossible to pen a personal portrait of a man dead nearly eight and a half centuries. Nevertheless, something of the man may be discerned mainly from his actions and also from the quills of contemporary, if often less judgemental, writers. We have no description of him, no effigy or likeness, so we have no way of knowing what he looked like, or how tall or short he was, or, indeed, if he was thin or fat. In stark contrast we have been left a vivid picture of Owain's son Rhun who is described as

> tall, and his flesh white, with curly flaxen hair, a long face, large, merry, blue eyes, a long stout neck, a broad chest, a long waist, stout thighs, long legs, long slender feet, long straight toes.[15]

Might it be a case of like father like son, for it is interesting that Owain's mother, Angharad, is described as having flaxen hair? Those whom he patronised were likely unconcerned with his physical appearance so long as they benefited from his bounty. Owain was a generous patron of native literature and the arts in general and of the bards in particular who repaid him by euolgising him in life as well as in death. Poetic material was extremely malleable and, carefully used, it could serve the cause of the patron. Poetic verses could be used to enhance the reputation of the patron, but also to undermine the morale of adversaries for propaganda purposes. The eloquent elegies of Daniel ap Llosgwrn, Seisyll Bryffwrch and especially Cynddelw Brydydd Mawr, of whom it has been said that 'his poetic gifts are seen at their height in the "Elegy to Owain," in 1170', speak of a man worthy of praise beyond the ordinary.[16]

Strip away the bardic hyperbole and what remains is a man of flesh and blood and one truly possessed of exceptional qualities. His defiance of the pope and the archbishop of Canterbury when called upon to put away his second wife, Cristin, suggests a man utterly devoted to his spouse. On the other hand, it may simply have been a case of a stubborn man refusing to yield to pressure applied by outsiders. Indeed, it must not be forgotten that Owain had several children by other women, which betokens a man of exceptional libido and scant regard for familial ties. The fact that a rift developed between Owain and his court poet, Gwlachmai ap Meilyr, again points to a man of fiery temperament. What caused these two to quarrel is not known but that a relationship which had endured for some years should end in bitter recrimination is evidence of a forceful and unforgiving personality. In spite of Gwalchmai's pleas to heal the rift, as far as is known the two were never reconciled.

He may have been exceptional but, clearly, he was also human and from the meagre evidence available he does seem to have been an emotional man, perhaps even prone to bouts of melancholia. The deaths of his son Rhun in 1146, and mother Angharad in 1162 provide brief glimpses of the man behind the mask. Of Rhun's death one cannot fail to be struck by the care taken by the chroniclers in composing an unusually long eulogy for a young man who had yet to truly make his mark on the world. Their words convey the consuming grief that a father felt for the sudden death of a beloved and promising son about to enter the most significant phase of his young adulthood:

'Making a good end': Death and Reputation

> When news of his death reached Owain, he fell into so great a sorrow that neither the splendour of sovereignty nor the entertainment of bards nor the solace of courtiers nor the sight of costly objects could raise him from his conceived sorrow and grief.[17]

There is even a hint that Owain's deep depression was serious and might have led to more than merely rendering him impotent in public affairs: 'as unbearable sorrow had disturbed the prince's mind and brought it low, even so did divine providence raise it up' for God 'saw good to show mercy to the race of the Britons… and He preserved Owain for them as leader'.[18] Personal grief struck him again 16 years later when 'Angharad, wife of Gruffudd, died. And therefore Owain ap Gruffudd conceived sorrow for the death of his mother so that nothing could cheer him'.[19]

Owain was sustained in his grief by the strength of his piety for he seems to have been a deeply religious man, beyond what historians like to describe as conventionally pious. He was a friend and patron of the church and those clerics whom he patronised repaid his faith in them by serving and supporting him in the face of intense pressure applied by king, pope and archbishop. His defence of the church in north Wales was not simply a cynical political ploy to enhance his power and status, though it did just that, it was equally a means by which its independence could be established and maintained. It is likely that religious and cultural sensitivity, underpinned by a strong sense of local pride and identity, played their part in Owain's attempt to promote and shape the church in Gwynedd. Unlike his father and brother, Owain appears not to have been a conspicuous patron of continental monasticism which suggests that he remained true to the native *clas* churches. This is not to suggest that Owain's father and brother abandoned the native church in favour of the new monastic movements: while Cadwaladr patronised the Augustinian abbey of Haughmond alongside the *clas* community at Tywyn, his father, Gruffudd, extended his largesse to include the Benedictine houses of Chester and Shrewsbury, and the native foundations within Gwynedd of Bangor, Bardsey, Caer Gybi, Clynnog Fawr and Penmon.

The only alien monastic house to come under Owain's control during his reign was the Cistercian abbey of Basingwerk. Established in 1131 or 1132, the community of Cistercian (formerly Savigniac) monks enjoyed the patronage of their founders, the earls of Chester, until 1167 when they came under the control of Owain Gwynedd. What transpired in the three years they laboured under Welsh control is not known but the fact that they remained in the house – there is no evidence of their eviction – suggests that they were at least tolerated if not patronised. As far as A.D. Carr is concerned, the best that can be said in respect of Owain's patronage of the native church is that 'it cannot be without significance that the priory church at Penmon, the tower at Llaneilian and part of the parish church of Aberffraw all date from this period'.[20] Nevertheless, it may be significant that, at his death, Owain followed his father, Gruffudd (as did Cadwaladr), in choosing to be buried in the cathedral church of Bangor, the site of a native *clas* community of canons.[21]

Owain Gwynedd was a leading figure in Wales for over 30 years during which time he earned the respect of his peers and established a reputation for fearlessness in war, wisdom in peace, ruthlessness in politics, prudence and moderation

'Making a good end': Death and Reputation

in governance. Thus did Cynddelw Brydydd Mawr laud a patron who was:

> Gentle towards the gentle in the peaceful countryside,
> rough towards the rough at the clash of arms,
> sweet towards the sweet at the recounting of his greatness,
> bitter towards the bitter when strife is sought.[22]

Not surprisingly, he soon acquired the epithet Fawr or Great, and among the first to refer to his greatness, outside the ranks of the bardic élite, was none other than Gerald of Wales.[23] In the opinion of Sir J.E. Lloyd it is 'a description he fully deserved' because his 'greatness was recognised alike by bard and by chronicler, by Welshman and Englishman, and among his eulogists are Archbishop Thomas of Canterbury'.[24]

Clearly it was not only contemporary bards and chroniclers who lavished praise on Owain Gwynedd. Modern historians too have afforded him a degree of approbation unusual in its generosity. According to A.D. Carr, Owain was 'one of the greatest members of a dynasty whose history is the history of independent Wales'.[25]

The late T. Jones Pierce was no less impressed by Owain, of whom he stated with undisguised pride in a fellow Welshman, that the

> praises so repeatedly accorded to his many personal qualities by contemporary poets, and indeed by several public figures who could not have been predisposed in his favour, have so genuine a tone about them that the progressive trends in all the arts of peace and war discerned in 12th cent. Wales, it must be concluded, were in large measure due to the fostering genius of 'Owain the Great'.[26]

No less laudatory is the opinion of the late Gwynfor Evans who, as befitting the former leader of the Welsh Nationalist Party, Plaid Cymru, regarded Owain Gwynedd as a great Welshman:

> Of the exceptionally able series of princes during the 12th and 13th centuries, including Llywelyn the Great, the Lord Rhys and Llywelyn ap Gruffudd, none was greater than Owain.[27]

In a fitting tribute to Owain ap Gruffudd ap Cynan, Sir J.E. Lloyd said 'Welsh history can scarcely show a nobler or a better-balanced character'.[28] Owain and his nemesis, Henry II, were so evenly matched, if not alike, that Lewis Warren's description of the Angevin may fairly be applied to the Venedotian:

> [Owain] was not superhuman. He had the frailties and passions of ordinary men – but in larger measure. He was no God-like Achilles, either in valour or in wrath; but in cunning and ingenuity, in fortitude and courage, he stands not far below the subtle-souled Odysseus.[29]

Notes

Preface

1. Paul Barbier, *The Age of Owain Gwynedd* (London, 1908), iii.
2. J. Beverley Smith, *Llywelyn ap Gruffudd Prince of Wales* (Cardiff, 1998).
3. Barbier, *Age of Owain Gwynedd*, 129.

Chapter I: The Gwynedd of Gruffudd ap Cynan

1. *Brenhinedd y Saeson or The Kings of the Saxons.* Translated with introduction and notes by Thomas Jones (Cardiff, 1971), 77. [Hereafter *B.Saes*]
2. *The Anglo-Saxon Chronicle.* Translated and edited by M.J. Swanton (London, 1996), 191.
3. *Annales Cambriae*, ed. J. Williams ab Ithel (Rolls Series, 1860), 25; *Brut y Tywysogyon or The Chronicle of the Princes. Red Book of Hergest Version.* Translated with introduction and notes by Thomas Jones (Cardiff, 1955), 27. [Hereafter *BTRBH*]
4. Frank Barlow, *The Godwins* (London, 2002), 57.
5. J.E. Lloyd, *A History of Wales* (2 vols, London, 1911), II, 373.
6. Marjorie Chibnall, *The Ecclesiastical History of Orderic Vitalis* (6 vols, Oxford, 1969–80), VI, 454, 456. [Hereafter *Orderic Vitalis*]
7. D. Simon Evans (ed. and trans.), *A Mediaeval Prince of Wales: The Life of Gruffudd ap Cynan* (Lampeter, 1990).
8. David Moore, 'Gruffudd ap Cynan and the Medieval Welsh Polity', in K.L. Maund, (ed.), *Gruffudd ap Cynan: A Collaborative Biography* (Woodbridge, 1996), 4–5.
9. David E. Thornton, 'Owain ab Edwin (d. 1105), ruler in Wales', *New Oxford Dictionary of National Biography*, online edition. [Hereafter *NODNB*]
10. *Orderic Vitalis*, IV, 138–9, 144–5; Evans, *The Life of Gruffudd ap Cynan*, 69.
11. *Brut y Tywysogyon or The Chronicle of the Princes. Peniarth Ms 20 Version.* Translated with introduction and notes by Thomas Jones (Cardiff, 1952), 19. [Hereafter *BTPen*]
12. For a fuller discussion of this disputed identification and the problems in dating, see David Moore, *op. cit.*, 36–9 and C.P Lewis, 'Gruffudd ap Cynan and the Normans' in Maund, (ed.), *Gruffudd ap Cynan: A Collaborative Biography*, 70–1.

13 R.R. Davies, *Conquest, Coexistence and Change Wales 1063–1415* (Oxford, 1987), 30; Huw Pryce, 'Gruffudd ap Cynan (1054/5–1137), King of Gwynedd', *NODNB*, online edition.
14 Evans, *The Life of Gruffudd ap Cynan*, 71, 73. At one point Gruffudd had 120 men and 'fourteen youths' in his employ.
15 *Ibid.*, 73.
16 *BTPen.*, 21. This might also have included Arfon, a region with which Gruffudd was closely associated.
17 Evans, *The Life of Gruffudd ap Cynan*, 79.
18 Davies, *Wales 1063–1415*, 40.
19 R.R. Davies, 'Henry I and Wales', in H. Mayr-Harting and R.I. Moore (eds.), *Studies in Medieval History presented to R.H.C. Davis* (London, 1985), 139.
20 *BTPen.*, 49.
21 *Ibid.*, 37.
22 *Ibid.*, 38. *The Anglo-Saxon Chronicle*, 245.
23 Quoted in C. Warren Hollister, *Henry I* (Yale, 2001), 369.
24 *BTPen.*, 39.
25 *Ibid.*, 39.
26 *Ibid.*, 39.
27 *BTRBH*, 105.
28 Evans, *The Life of Gruffudd ap Cynan*, 81.
29 Lewis, *op.cit.*, 58.
30 *Ibid.*
31 Evans, *The Life of Gruffudd ap Cynan*, 81.
32 *BTPen.*, 52.

Chapter II: 'Unconquered from his youth': Royal Apprenticeship

1 Lloyd, *History of Wales*, II, 464.
2 J. Beverley Smith, 'Owain Gwynedd', *Transactions of the Caernarfonshire Historical Society*, Vol. 32 (1971), 8.
3 *BTPen.*, 49; *BTRBH*, 109; *B.Saes.*, 141.
4 Sean Davies, *Welsh Military Institutions 633–1283* (Cardiff, 2004), 74.
5 Barbier, *Age of Owain Gwynedd*, 15.
6 Lloyd, *History of Wales*, II, 466 n.15.
7 Lloyd, *ibid.*, II, 476. In fact Lloyd's narrative strongly suggests that Ceredigion was divided up between Cadwaladr ap Gruffudd and his nephew Hywel ab Owain Gwynedd as early as 1138. This impression is repeated in Lloyd's *The Story of Ceredigion* (Cardiff, 1937), 57–8.

Notes

8   David Moore, 'Gruffudd ap Cynan and the Medieval Welsh Polity' in Maund, (ed.), *Gruffudd ap Cynan*, 13.

9   *Ibid.*, 13.

10 Tony Conran, *Welsh Verse* (Bridgend, 1992), 186. A phrase translated from Iolo Goch's poem addressed to Owain Glyndŵr. J.E. Lloyd has rendered the line into English thus 'A goodly nestful of young princes' in *Owen Glendower* (Oxford, 1931), 27.

11 J.E. Caerwyn Williams, 'Meilyr Brydydd and Gruffudd ap Cynan' in Maund (ed.), *Gruffudd ap Cynan*, 174. Tellingly, later in the same poem, it is as 'The lord of Môn' that Gruffudd is described by his chief poet. *Ibid.*, 185.

12 *BTRBH*, 39.

13 *BTPen.*, 62.

14 *Ibid.*, 169.

15 Evans, *The Life of Gruffudd ap Cynan*, 11.

16 Walter Map, *De Nugis Curialium*, ed. M.R. James, C.N.L. Brooke and R.A.B. Mynors (Oxford, 1985), 476. William of Malmesbury, *Gesta Regum Anglorum*, ed. and trans., R.A.B. Mynors, R.M. Thompson and M. Winterbottom (2 vols, Oxford, 1998–9), II, 467.

17 V.H. Galbraith, 'The Literacy of the Medieval English Kings', in *Idem., Kings and Chronicles: Essays in English Medieval History* (London, 1982), 90–1.

18 R. Geraint Gruffydd, 'Gogynfeirdd', *NODNB online edition*.

19 *BTPen.*, 49.

20 Katherine Anderson, 'Urth Noe e Tat: The Question of Fosterage in High Medieval Wales', *North American Journal of Welsh Studies*, 4:1 (2004), 9.

21 For the debate on Welsh fosterage, see Katherine Anderson, *NAJWS* (2004), 1–11; Christopher McAll, 'The Normal Paradigms of a Woman's Life in the Irish and Welsh Law Texts', in *The Welsh Law of Women*, eds., Dafydd Jenkins and Morfydd Owen (Cardiff, 1980), 7–22; Llinos Beverley Smith, 'Fosterage, Adoption and God-Parenthood: Ritual and Fictive Kinship in Medieval Wales', *Welsh History Review*, 16 (1992), 1–35 and Thomas Glyn Watkins, *The Legal History of Wales* (Cardiff, 2007), 56.

22 Evans, *Life of Gruffudd ap Cynan*, 28; For Hywel ab Owain Gwynedd, see Anderson, *op. cit.*, 6–7.

23 Gerald of Wales, *The Journey through Wales and the Description of Wales*, trans. Lewis Thorpe (Harmondsworth, 1978), 261.

24 A.W. Wade-Evans, *Welsh Medieval Law* (Oxford, 1909), 138.

25 David Stephenson, *The Governance of Gwynedd* (Cardiff, 1984), 138.

26 Evans, *Life of Gruffudd ap Cynan*, 82.

27 David Moore, *op. cit.*, 17.

28 Evans, *Life of Gruffudd ap Cynan*, 83.

Chapter III: 'Victories beyond number': War, Conquest and Expansion

1 B.Saes., 145.
2 J. Beverley Smith, 'Owain Gwynedd', *Trans. Caern. Hist. Soc.*, 32, 8; K. Maund, *The Welsh Kings* (Stroud, 2000), 98.
3 Lloyd, *History of Wales*, II, 467.
4 Maund, *The Welsh Kings*, 97.
5 *BTRBH*, 115; *BTPen.,* 51; Humphrey Llwyd, *Cronica Walliae*, ed. Ieuan William (Cardiff, 2002), 150.
6 *BTPen.,* 51.
7 This refers to the Viking origins of the Normans. Early in the tenth century the area known as Normandy was ceded to these formidable northern warriors who settled and established the most powerful duchy in France. For a brief, reliable guide, see Trevor Rowley, *The Normans* (Stroud, 1999).
8 David Walker, *The Norman Conquerors* (Swansea, 1977), 45.
9 *BTPen.,* 42.
10 Hollister, *Henry I*, 132.
11 *Ibid.*, 339.
12 *BTRBH*, 71.
13 Lloyd, *The Story of Ceredigion*, 44.
14 Quoted in Walker, *The Norman Conquerors*, 47. Coed Grono or Grwyne is in the vicinity of Crickhowell.
15 *Ibid*. Richard's widow, Adeliza, would remain trapped in Cardigan Castle for some months until rescued by Miles of Gloucester at the end of the year.
16 *BTPen.,* 51.
17 Gerald of Wales, *Journey and Description of Wales*, 267.
18 *Ibid.*, 177.
19 *Ibid.*
20 *BTPen.,* 51.
21 Quoted in Sean Davies, *Welsh Military Institutions*, 221. See also, K.R. Potter and R.H.C. Davis (ed. and trans.), *Gesta Stephani* (Oxford, 1976), 17–19. [Hereafter *Gesta Stephani*]
22 Lloyd, *History of Wales*, II, 476.
23 David Crouch argues persuasively that the idea that Stephen's reign was rent by anarchy should be discarded. See his, *The Reign of King Stephen, 1135–1154* (London, 2000). On the other hand, see E. King (ed.), *The Anarchy of King Stephen's Reign* (Oxford, 1994).
24 *Gesta Stephani*, 14–16.
25 *Symeonis Historia Regnum Constinuata per Johannem Hagustaldensem*, in *Historia Regum*, ed. T. Arnold (London, 1885), ii, 287.

Notes

26 Lloyd, *History of Wales*, II, 479.
27 *Orderic Vitalis*, VI, 494.
28 *Ibid.*, II, 489.
29 For the size of the *teulu*, see Davies, *Welsh Military Institutions*, 22–6. See also, A.D. Carr, 'Teulu and Penteulu', in T.M. Charles-Edwards *et al.* (eds.), *The Welsh King and his Court* (Cardiff, 2000), 63–81.
30 Orderic Vitalis's reference to a Maredudd, brother of Cadwaladr, seems to fit Madog ap Maredudd who was his brother-in-law but David Crouch has suggested that this Maredudd might be Cadwaladr's son. *Orderic Vitalis*, VI, 536; Crouch, *Reign of King Stephen*, 142 n.22. See also D. Crouch, 'The March and the Welsh Kings', in *The Anarchy of King Stephen's Reign*, 255–89.
31 *Historia Regnum... Johannem Hagustaldensem*, ii, 307.
32 *Gesta Stephani*, 173.
33 *Orderic Vitalis*, VI, 536.
34 *BTRBH*, 111.
35 *Ibid.*, 129.
36 T. Wright (ed.), *A Selection of Latin Stories* (Percy Society, 8, 1842), 36.
37 *Gesta Stephani*, 18.

Chapter IV: 'Slayers of their enemies': Owain and Cadwaladr

1 *BTRBH*, 113, 115.
2 *Orderic Vitalis*, VI, 536.
3 Lloyd, *History of Wales*, II, 469.
4 J. Goronwy Edwards, *Littere Wallie* (Cardiff, 1940), xxxvi.
5 *Ibid.*, xxxvii. Edwards admits in theory to the indivisibility of the kingship but states that this did not operate in the political reality of the period.
6 Crouch, *Reign of King Stephen*, 246.
7 J. Beverley Smith, 'Owain Gwynedd', *Trans. Caern. Hist. Soc.*, 32, 13; idem., *Llywelyn ap Gruffudd*, 8.
8 J. Beverley Smith, 'Owain Gwynedd', *Trans. Caern. Hist. Soc.*, 32, 13. See also 'The Age of the Princes' in J. Beverley Smith and Llinos Beverley Smith (eds.), *History of Merioneth. The Middle Ages.* Vol. 2 (Cardiff, 2001).
9 Huw Pryce, 'Cadwaladr ap Gruffudd (d. 1172)', *NODNB, online edition*.
10 *BTPen.*, 53.
11 *BTRBH*, 119.
12 *BTPen.*, 53.
13 *Cronica Walliae*, 153.
14 *BTRBH*, 127.

15   *BTPen.*, 57.
16   *Cronica Walliae*, 156.
17   *BTPen.*, 58.
18   *Cronica Walliae*, 157.
19   *Ibid.*, 157–8.
20   For a comprehensive debate of the source evidence available to and used by Llwyd, see *Cronica Walliae*, 1–59.
21   The identification of Cadwaladr's wife 'Aliz de Clare' with Adeliza de Clare is not certain but is generally accepted to be correct. The only possible alternative is that she was the daughter rather than the widow of Richard de Clare and thus a niece of Earl Ranulf.
22   *The Charters of the Anglo-Norman Earls of Chester c. 1071–1237*, ed. G. Barraclough (Record Society of Lancashire and Cheshire, 126 (1988), nos. 28, 64, 84–5.
23   Huw Pryce, 'Owain Gwynedd [Owain ap Gruffudd] (d. 1170), King of Gwynedd', *NODNB, online edition.*
24   Lloyd, *History of Wales*, II, 496.
25   Davies, *Welsh Military Institutions*, 230.
26   Lloyd, *History of Wales*, II, 488, 489.

Chapter V: A test of strength: Owain and Henry II

1   W.L. Warren, *Henry II* (London, 1973), 630.
2   *BTRBH*, 179.
3   Davies, *Wales 1063–1415*, 48.
4   Quoted in M.T. Clanchy, *England and its Rulers 1066–1272* (2nd edn, Oxford, 1998), 88
5   Davies, *Wales 1063–1415*, 51.
6   *Ibid.*, 51.
7   *BTPen.*, 59.
8   *Ibid.*
9   Warren, *Henry II*, 69–70.
10   *Ibid.*, 70.
11   *The Historical Works of Gervase of Canterbury*, ed. W. Stubbs (2 vols, London, 1879–80), I, 165.
12   *BTRBH.*, 135.
13   *B.Saes.*, 159.
14   *BTPen.*, 60. The Henry killed in battle was the illegitimate son of Henry I.
15   Gerald of Wales, *Journey and Description of Wales*, 189.

Notes

16 *Chronicles of the Reigns of Stephen, Henry II and Richard I*, ed. R. Howlett (4 vols, London, 1884–9), IV, 195.

17 R.R. Davies, *Domination and Conquest: the experience of Ireland, Scotland and Wales* (Cambridge, 1990), 54.

18 *BTRBH.*, 143.

19 Lloyd, *History of Wales*, II, 512.

20 *Radulfi de Diceto Decani Lundoniensis Opera Historica*, ed. W. Stubbs (2 vols, London, 1876), I, 311.

21 Warren, *Henry II*, 163.

22 Davies, *Wales 1063–1415*, 52.

23 *BTPen.*, 60.

24 *Ibid.*

25 *Materials for the History of Thomas Becket, Archbishop of Canterbury*, ed. J.C. Robertson (7 vols, London, 1875–85), VII, 124. [Hereafter *MTB*]

26 Warren, *Henry II*, 217. *Historia gloriosi Regis Ludovici VII* (History of the glorious king Louis VII), ed. A. Molinier (Paris, 1887), 161.

27 *B.Saes.*, 165.

28 Warren, *Henry II*, 210, 211.

29 *BTPen.*, 63.

30 *BTPen.*, 63; *B.Saes.*, 165; *BTRBH.*, 147; *Annales Cambriae*, 50.

31 Paul Latimer, 'Henry II's Campaign against the Welsh in 1165', *WHR*, 14 (1989), 536.

32 *Chronicles of the Reigns of Stephen, Henry II and Richard I*, I, 145.

33 David Carpenter, *The Struggle for Mastery: Britain 1066–1284* (London, 2003), 214. 'Apart from the Toulouse campaign'.

34 Ralph of Coggeshall, *Chronicon Anglicanum*, ed. J. Stevenson (London, 1875), 25–6.

35 *Ibid.*, 25.

36 Gerald of Wales, *Journey and Description of Wales*, 197.

Chapter VI: 'Faithful and devoted friends': Owain and Louis VII

This chapter derives its inspiration from, and owes a considerable debt to, the pioneering work undertaken by Professor Huw Pryce of Bangor University.

1 H. Pryce, 'Owain Gwynedd and Louis VII: The Franco-Welsh Diplomacy of the First Prince of Wales', *WHR*, 19 (1998), 4 [in translation], 26 [in Latin].

2 *MTB*, V, 49.

3 Sean Duffy, 'Henry II and England's Insular Neighbours', in C. Harper-Bill and N. Vincent (eds.), *Henry II: New Interpretations* (Woodbridge, 2007), 134; Pryce, 'Owain Gwynedd', *WHR*, 19, 4–5.

4   J. Beverley Smith, Owain Gwynedd', *Trans. Caern. Hist. Soc.*, 32, 16.
5   Pryce, 'Owain Gwynedd', *WHR*, 19, 7 [in translation], 27 [in Latin].
6   *Ibid.*, 4 [in translation], 26 [in Latin].
7   *Ibid.*
8   J. Gillingham, 'Doing Homage to the King of France', in C. Harper-Bill and N. Vincent (eds.), *Henry II: New Interpretations*, 73.
9   Pryce, 'Owain Gwynedd', *WHR*, 19, 4 [in translation], 26 [in Latin].
10 *Chronicles of the Reigns of Stephen, Henry II and Richard I*, IV, 222.
11 Pryce, 'Owain Gwynedd', *WHR*, 19, 6 [in translation], 27 [in Latin].
12 *Ibid.*, 7 [in translation], 28 [in Latin].
13 *Ibid.*, 7 [in translation], 27 [in Latin].
14 *Ibid.*
15 *Ibid.*, 7 [in translation], 27–8 [in Latin].
16 *Ibid.*, 8 [in translation], 28 [in Latin].
17 *Ibid.*, 7 [in translation], 28 [in Latin].
18 Gerald of Wales, *Journey and Description of Wales*, 267.
19 *Ibid.*
20 Quoted in Warren, *Henry II*, 628–9. For the original letter, see *The Letters of Arnulf of Lisieux*, ed. F. Barlow (Camden Society, LXI, 1939), no. 42.
21 Pryce, 'Owain Gwynedd', *WHR*, 19, 19.
22 *The Letters of John of Salisbury*, ed. W.J. Millor, H.E. Butler and C.N.L. Brooke (2 vols, London, 1955–79), II, 606.
23 Lloyd, *Hist. Wales*, II, 607.

Chapter VII: 'Equity, prudence and princely moderation': Politics, Power and Princely Rule

1   Gerald of Wales, *Journey and Description of Wales*, 203.
2   Clanchy, *England and its Rulers*, 107.
3   *BTRBH*, 115.
4   David Moore, 'Gruffudd ap Cynan and the Medieval Welsh Polity' in Maund, (ed.), *Gruffudd ap Cynan*, 55, 56.
5   Lloyd, *Hist. Wales*, II, 416.
6   W.E. Davies, *Wales in the Early Middle Ages* (Leicester, 1982), 106.
7   Davies, *Wales 1063–1415*, 12.
8   Evans, *The Life of Gruffudd ap Cynan*, 81.
9   *BTRBH*, 117.
10 *BTRBH*, 151; *Cronica Walliae*, 167.
11 *BTRBH*, 115.

Notes

12 Sean Davies, *Welsh Military Institutions*, 83.
13 *BTPen.*, 53; *B.Saes.*, 149.
14 Richard Avent, *Castles of the Princes of Gwynedd* (Cardiff, 1983), 5.
15 A.H.A. Hogg and D.J.C. King, 'Early Castles in Wales and the Marches: a preliminary list', *Archaeologia Cambrensis*, CXII (1963), 77–124. See also, D.J.C. King, *Castellarium Anglicanum* (2 vols, London, 1983).
16 Evans, *The Life of Gruffudd ap Cynan*, 82–3.
17 Gerald of Wales, *Journey and Description of Wales*, 223; Neil Johnstone, '*Llys* and *maerdref*: the royal courts of the princes of Gwynedd: A study of their location and selective trial excavation', *Studia Celtica*, 34 (2000), 167–210; David Longley, 'The Royal Courts of the Welsh Princes in Gwynedd, AD 400–1283', in Nancy Edwards (ed.), *Landscape and Settlement in Medieval Wales* (Oxford, 1997), 41–54.
18 Evans, *The Life of Gruffudd ap Cynan*, 61.
19 *BTRBH.*, 119.
20 *BTPen.*, 59.
21 Evans, *The Life of Gruffudd ap Cynan*, 59.
22 H. Pryce, *Native Law and the Church in Medieval Wales* (Oxford, 1993), 242.
23 M. Chibnall, *Anglo-Norman England 1066–1166* (Oxford, 1986), 121.
24 Davies, *Wales, 1063–1415*, 254.
25 Stephenson, *The Governance of Gwynedd*, 24.
26 H. Pryce, *The Acts of the Welsh Rulers 1120–1283* (Cardiff, 2005), 322–3. Owain's letter to Bernard, bishop of St David's is of dubious authenticity because the only copy is preserved in Gerald of Wales's *De Invectionibus*. However, Professor Pryce states that 'the balance of probability is against its being an outright fabrication'.
27 *Ibid.*, 70–1.
28 *Ibid.*, 322.
29 *The Correspondence of Thomas Becket, Archbishop of Canterbury, 1162–1170*, ed. Anne Duggan (2 vols, Oxford, 2000), I, 235, 239: Pryce, *Acts of the Welsh Rulers*, 324–5.
30 Duggan, *Correspondence of Thomas Becket*, I, 33.
31 *Ibid.*, II, 875, 973, 977.
32 *The Cartulary of Haughmond Abbey*, ed. Una Rees (Cardiff, 1985), no. 784 f.149r; Pryce, *Acts of the Welsh Rulers*, 329–31.
33 Pryce, 'Owain Gwynedd', *WHR*, 19, 17.
34 *Ibid.*, 8, 17.
35 *BTRBH.*, 131.
36 *BT Pen.*, 58.

37 Lloyd, *Hist. Wales*, II, 483.
38 *Ibid.*
39 *Episcopal Acts relating to Welsh Dioceses, 1066–1272*, ed. J. Conway Davies (2 vols, Historical Society of the Church in Wales, 1946–8), II, 416.
40 Pryce, *Acts of the Welsh Rulers*, 322–3.
41 Glanmor Williams, *The Welsh Church from Conquest to Reformation* (2nd edn, Cardiff, 1976), 4.
42 Duggan, *Correspondence of Thomas Becket*, I, 235.
43 *Ibid.*, II, 841.
44 *Ibid.*
45 *Ibid.*, II, 977.
46 *Ibid.*, II, 841.
47 *Ibid.*, II, 875.

Chapter VIII: 'Making a good end': Death and Reputation
1 *BTRBH.*, 151.
2 *BTPen.*, 63; *BTRBH.*, 145.
3 Barbier, *Age of Owain Gwynedd*, 15.
4 R.G. Gruffydd (ed.), *Cyfres Beirdd y Tywysogion* (7 Vols, Cardiff, 1991–6), I, 73–5; G. Williams, *Welsh Poems, Sixth century to 1600* (London, 1973), 35; Conran, *Welsh Verse*, 143–4.
5 Duggan, *Correspondence of Thomas Becket*, II, 875.
6 Gerald of Wales, *Journey and Description of Wales*, 203.
7 *Ibid.*, 202.
8 *The Autobiography of Gerald of Wales*, ed. and trans. by H.E. Butler (new edn, 2005), 57.
9 *BTRBH.*, 151.
10 The carving may have been similar to that applied to the flat capstone of Joan's tomb still to be seen at Beaumaris Church. The wife of Owain's grandson, Llywelyn the Great, she died in 1237.
11 Gerald of Wales, *Journey and Description of Wales*, 192.
12 *Ibid.*
13 *Ibid.*
14 Smith, *Llywelyn ap Gruffudd*, 283.
15 *BTPen.*, 55.
16 R.T. Jenkins *et al.* (ed.), *Dictionary of Welsh Biography* (London, 1959), 90.
17 *BTPen.*, 55.
18 *Ibid.*

Notes

19 *BTRBH.*, 163.
20 A.D. Carr, *Medieval Anglesey* (Llangefni, 1982), 43.
21 David Crouch, *The Image of Aristocracy in Britain* (London, 1992), 338
22 A.O.H Jarman & G.R. Hughes (eds.), *A Guide to Welsh Literature* (2 vols, Swansea, 1976; repr., 1979), I, 170.
23 Of course we must bear in mind that Owain *Fawr* or Owain *Magnus* can be interpreted as 'the elder' rather than 'the Great', but such was the aura of greatness surrounding the man, as reported by contemporaries, that the latter is preferred here.
24 Lloyd, *Hist. Wales*, II, 488.
25 A.D. Carr, *Medieval Wales* (1995), 42.
26 *Dictionary of Welsh Biography*, 693.
27 Gwynfor Evans, *Welsh Nation Builders* (Llandysul, 1988), 77.
28 Lloyd, *Hist. Wales*, II, 488.
29 Warren, *Henry II*, 630.

Bibliography

This book is based, as far as possible, on original sources most of them translated from Latin and Welsh. This is a highly selective and brief guide to works of use on the general topics covered by each of the chapters.

Anderson, Katherine, 'Urth Noe e Tat: The Question of Fosterage in High Medieval Wales', *North American Journal of Welsh Studies*, 4:1 (2004), 1–11.

The Anglo-Saxon Chronicle. Translated and edited by M.J. Swanton (London, 1996).

Annales Cambriae, ed. J. Williams ab Ithel (Rolls Series, 1860).

The Autobiography of Giraldus Cambrensis, ed. H.E. Butler (rev. edn, Woodbridge, 2005).

Avent, Richard, *Cestyll Tywysogion Gwynedd: Castles of the princes of Gwynedd* (Cardiff, 1983).

Avent, Richard, 'Castles of the Welsh princes', *Château Gaillard*, 16 (1992).

Barbier, P., *The Age of Owain Gwynedd* (London, 1908).

Barlow, Frank, *The Godwins* (London, 2002).

Benson, R.L. & Constable, G. (ed.), *Renaissance and Renewal in the Twelfth Century* (Oxford, 1982).

Harper-Bill, C. and Vincent, N. (eds.), *Henry II: New Interpretations* (Woodbridge, 2007).

Binchy, D.A., *Celtic and Anglo-Saxon Kingship* (Oxford, 1970).

Binns, A., *Dedications to Monastic Houses in England and Wales* (Woodbridge, 1989).

Bramley, K.A., et al. (eds.). *Gwaith Llywelyn Fardd I ac eraill o feirdd y ddeuddegfed ganrif* [The works of Llywelyn Fardd and other twelfth-century poets] (Cardiff, 1994).

Brenhinedd y Saeson or The Kings of the Saxons. Translated with introduction and notes by Thomas Jones (Cardiff, 1971).

Brut y Tywysogyon or The Chronicle of the Princes. Peniarth Ms 20 Version. Translated with introduction and notes by Thomas Jones (Cardiff, 1952).

Brut y Tywysogyon or The Chronicle of the Princes. Red Book of Hergest Version. Translated with introduction and notes by Thomas Jones (Cardiff, 1955).

Bibliography

Carpenter, D.A., *The Struggle for Mastery: Britain 1066–1284* (London, 2003).

Carr, A.D., *Medieval Anglesey* (Llangefni, 1982).

Carr, A.D. 'Anglo-Welsh relations, 1066–1282', in Jones, M. C. E. Vale, Malcolm Graham Allan (ed.), *England and her neighbours, 1066–1453: Essays in Honour of Pierre Chaplais* (London, 1989).

Carr, A.D., *Medieval Wales* (London, 1995).

Carr, A.D., 'Llywelyn ab Iorwerth', *New Oxford Dictionary of National Biography*, online edition.

The Cartulary of Haughmond Abbey, ed. Una Rees (Cardiff, 1985).

The Charters of the Anglo-Norman Earls of Chester c.1071–1237, ed. G. Barraclough (Record Society of Lancashire and Cheshire, 126; 1988).

Chibnall, Marjorie, *The Ecclesiastical History of Orderic Vitalis* (6 vols, Oxford, 1969–80).

Chibnall, Marjorie, *Anglo-Norman England 1066–1166* (Oxford, 1986).

Chronicles of the Reigns of Stephen, Henry II and Richard I, ed. R. Howlett (4 vols, London, 1884–9).

Church, S. D. (ed.). *King John: new interpretations* (Woodbridge, 1999).

Clanchy, M.T., *England and its Rulers 1066–1272* (2nd edn, Oxford, 1998).

Coggeshall, Ralph of, *Chronicon Anglicanum*, ed. J. Stevenson (London, 1875).

Conran, Tony, *Welsh Verse* (Bridgend, 1992).

The Correspondence of Thomas Becket, Archbishop of Canterbury, 1162–1170, ed. Anne Duggan (2 vols, Oxford, 2000).

Costigan, N. G., et al. (eds.), *Gwaith Dafydd Benfras ac eraill o feirdd hanner cyntaf y drydedd ganrif ar ddeg* [The works of Dafydd Benfras and other thirteenth-century poets] (Cardiff, 1995).

Crouch, David B., *William Marshal: court, career and chivalry in the Angevin Empire, 1147–1219* (London, 1990).

Crouch, David B., *The Image of Aristocracy in Britain 1000–1300* (1992).

Crouch, David B., *The Reign of King Stephen, 1135–1154* (London, 2000).

Davies, R.R., *Conquest, Coexistence and Change Wales 1063–1415* (Oxford, 1987).

Davies, R.R. (ed.), *The British Isles, 1150–1500: Comparisons, Contrasts and Connections* (Edinburgh, 1988).

Davies, R.R., *Domination and Conquest: the experience of Ireland, Scotland and Wales* (Cambridge, 1990).

Davies, R.R., 'Henry I and Wales', in H. Mayr-Harting and R.I. Moore (eds.), *Studies in Medieval History presented to R.H.C. Davis* (London, 1985).

Davies, Sean. *Welsh Military Institutions, 633–1283* (Cardiff, 2004).

Davies, W.E., *Wales in the Early Middle Ages* (Leicester, 1982).

Charles-Edwards, T.M., 'The Heir-Apparent in Irish and Welsh Law', *Celtica*, IX, 180–90.

Charles-Edwards, T.M. et al. (eds.), *The Welsh King and his Court* (Cardiff, 2000).

Edwards, J.G., *Littere Wallie* (Cardiff, 1940).

Edwards, J.G., 'The Royal Household in the Welsh Lawbooks', *TRHS*, XIII (1963), 163–76.

Episcopal Acts relating to Welsh Dioceses, 1066–1272, ed. J. Conway Davies (2 vols, Historical Society of the Church in Wales, 1946–8).

Wade-Evans, A.W., *Welsh Medieval Law* (Oxford, 1909).

Evans, D.S. (ed. and trans.), *A Mediaeval Prince of Wales: The Life of Gruffudd ap Cynan* (Lampeter, 1990).

Evans, Gwynfor, *Welsh Nation Builders* (Llandysul, 1988).

Galbraith, V.H., 'The Literacy of the Medieval English Kings', in Galbraith, V.H, *Kings and Chronicles: Essays in English Medieval History* (London, 1982).

Gruffydd, R.G. (ed.), *Cyfres Beirdd y Tywysogion* (7 Vols, Cardiff, 1991–6).

Hallam, E., 'Royal Burial and Cult of Kingship in Medieval England, 1060–1330', *Journal of Medieval History*, 8 (1982), 359–80.

The Historical Works of Gervase of Canterbury, ed. W. Stubbs (2 vols, London, 1879–80).

Historia gloriosi Regis Ludovici VII, ed. A. Molinier (Paris, 1887).

Hogg, A.H.A. and King, D.J.C., 'Early Castles in Wales and the Marches: a preliminary list', *Archaeologia Cambrensis*, CXII (1963), 77–124.

Howell, M., 'Regalian Rights in Wales and the March: the Relation of Theory to Practice', *Welsh History Review*, VII (1975), 269–88.

Insley, Charles, 'From *Rex Wallie* to *Princeps Wallie*: charters and state formation in thirteenth-century Wales', in Maddicott, J. R. Palliser, David Michael (ed.), *The Medieval State: Essays Presented to James Campbell* (London, 2000).

Insley, Charles, 'The wilderness years of Llywelyn the Great', in Prestwich, Michael, Britnell, Richard Hugh and Frame, Robin (ed.), *Thirteenth-Century England IX: Proceedings of the Durhan Conference, 2001* (Woodbridge, 2003).

Jack, R.I., *Medieval Wales* (London, 1972).

Jarman, A.O.H & Hughes, G.R. (eds.), *A Guide to Welsh Literature* (2 vols, Swansea, 1976; repr., 1979).

Jenkins, R.T. et al. (ed.), *Dictionary of Welsh Biography* (London, 1959).

Jenkins, D., 'Cynghellor and Chancellor', *Bulletin of Board of Celtic Studies*, XXVII (1976), 115–18.

Bibliography

Jenkins, D., 'Kings, Lords and Princes: the Nomenclature of Authority in Thirteenth-Century Wales', *Bulletin of Board of Celtic Studies*, XXVI (1976), 451–62.

Johnstone, N., '*Llys* and *maerdref*: the royal courts of the princes of Gwynedd: A study of their location and selective trial excavation', *Studia Celtica*, 34 (2000), 167–210.

Jolliffe, J.E.A., *Angevin Kingship* (London, 1963).

Jones, G.R.J., 'The Defences of Gwynedd in the Thirteenth Century', *Transactions of the Caernarfonshire Historical Society* (1969), 29–43.

Jones, N.A. & Pryce, H., *Yr Arglwydd Rhys* (Caerdydd, 1996).

King, D.J.C., *Castellarium Anglicanum: An Index and Bibliography of Castles in England* (London, 1983).

King, E. (ed.), *The Anarchy of King Stephen's Reign* (Oxford, 1994).

Knowles, D. & Hadcock, R.N., *Medieval Religious Houses. England and Wales* (2nd ed., London, 1971).

Koch, J.T., 'When was Welsh Literature first written down?', *Studia Celtica*, XX/XXI (1985–6), 43–66.

Latimer, Paul, 'Henry II's Campaign against the Welsh in 1165', *Welsh History Review*, 14 (1989), 536.

The Letters of Arnulf of Lisieux, ed. F. Barlow (Camden Society, LXI, 1939), no. 42.

The Letters of John of Salisbury, ed. W.J. Millor, H.E. Butler and C.N.L. 4. Brooke (2 vols, London, 1955–79).

Lloyd, J.E., *A History of Wales from earliest times to the Edwardian Conquest* (2 vols, 1911).

Lloyd, J.E., *The Story of Ceredigion* (Cardiff, 1937).

Llwyd, Humphrey, *Cronica Walliae*, ed. Ieuan M. Williams (Cardiff, 2002).

Longley, D., 'The Royal Courts of the Welsh Princes in Gwynedd, AD400–1283', in Nancy Edwards (ed.), *Landscape and Settlement in Medieval Wales* (Oxford, 1997), 41–54.

Map, Walter, *De Nugis Curialium*, ed. M.R. James, C.N.L. Brooke and R.A.B. Mynors (Oxford, 1985).

Materials for the History of Thomas Becket, Archbishop of Canterbury, ed. J.C. Robertson (7 vols, London, 1875–85).

Maund, K.L. (ed.), *Gruffudd ap Cynan: a collaborative biography* (Woodbridge, 1996).

Maund, K.L., *Handlist of the acts of native Welsh rulers, 1132–1283* (Cardiff, 1996).

Maund, K.L., *The Welsh Kings* (Stroud, 2000).

McAll, Christopher, 'The Normal Paradigms of a Woman's Life in the Irish and Welsh Law Texts', in *The Welsh Law of Women*, eds., Dafydd Jenkins and Morfydd Owen (Cardiff, 1980).

Pierce, T.J., *Medieval Welsh Society*, ed. J.B. Smith (Cardiff, 1972).

Potter, K.R. and Davis, R.H.C. (ed. and trans.), *Gesta Stephani* (Oxford, 1976).

Pryce, Huw, *Native law and the church in medieval Wales* (Oxford, 1993).

Pryce, Huw (ed.), *The Acts of Welsh Rulers, 1120–1283* (Cardiff, 2005).

Pryce, Huw, 'Owain Gwynedd and Louis VII: The Franco-Welsh Diplomacy of the First Prince of Wales', *Welsh History Review*, XIX (1998), 1–28.

Pryce, Huw, 'Gruffudd ap Cynan (1054/5–1137), King of Gwynedd', *New Oxford Dictionary of National Biography, online edition*.

Pryce, Huw, 'Owain Gwynedd [Owain ap Gruffudd] (d. 1170), King of Gwynedd', *New Oxford Dictionary of National Biography, online edition*.

Pryce, Huw. 'Culture, power and the charters of Welsh rulers', in Flanagan, Marie Therese and Green, Judith A. (ed.), *Charters and Charter Scholarship in Britain and Ireland* (Basingstoke, 2005), 184–202.

Radulfi de Diceto Decani Lundoniensis Opera Historica, ed. W. Stubbs (2 vols, London, 1876).

Richter, M., 'The Political and Institutional background to National Consciousness in Medieval Wales', in Moody, T.W. (ed.), *Nationality and the Pursuit of National Independence* (Belfast, 1978).

Roderick, A.J., 'The Feudal Relations between the English Crown and the Welsh Princes', *History*, XXXVII (1952), 210–12.

Roderick, A.J., 'Marriage and Politics in Wales, 1066–1282', *Welsh History Review*, IV (1968–9), 1–20.

Rowlands, I.W., 'King John and Wales', in Church, S.D. (ed.), *King John : new interpretations* (Woodbridge, 1999).

Rowley, Trevor, *The Normans* (Stroud, 1999).

Smith, J.B., *Llywelyn ap Gruffudd Prince of Wales* (Cardiff, 1998).

Smith, J. B. & Smith, L.B. (ed.), *History of Merioneth, volume II: The middle ages*. Cardiff, 2001).

Smith, J.B., 'Offra Principis Wallie Domino Regi', *Bulletin of the Board of Celtic Studies*, XXIV (1966), 362–7.

Smith, J.B., 'Owain Gwynedd', *Transactions of the Caernarfonshire Historical Society*, 32 (1971), 8–17.

Smith, L.B., 'Fosterage, Adoption and God-Parenthood: Ritual and Fictive Kinship in Medieval Wales', *Welsh History Review*, 16 (1992), 1–35.

Stephenson, D., *The Governance of Gwynedd* (Cardiff, 1984).

Bibliography

Symeonis Historia Regnum Constinuata per Johannem Hagustaldensem, in *Historia Regum*, ed. T. Arnold (London, 1885).

Thornton, D., 'Owain ab Edwin (d. 1105), ruler in Wales', *New Oxford Dictionary of National Biography*, online edition.

Treharne, R.F., 'The Franco-Welsh Treaty of alliance in 1212', *Bulletin of the Board of Celtic Studies*, XVIII (1958), 60–75.

Turvey, Roger, *The Lord Rhys Prince of Deheubarth* (Llandysul, 1997).

Turvey, Roger, *The Welsh Princes, 1063–1283* (London, 2002).

Turvey, Roger, *Llywelyn the Great* (Llandysul, 2007).

Wales, Gerald of, *The Journey through Wales and the Description of Wales*, trans. Lewis Thorpe (Harmondsworth, 1978).

Walker, D.G., *The Norman Conquerors* (Swansea, 1977).

Walker, D.G. (ed.), *A History of the Church in Wales* (Penarth, 1976; repr. 1991).

Walker, D.G., *Medieval Wales* (Cambridge, 1990; repr., 1994).

Warren, W.L., *Henry II* (London, 1973).

Warren, W.L., *King John* (2nd edn, London, 1978).

Watkins, T.G., *The Legal History of Wales* (Cardiff, 2007).

Williams, J.E.C., *The Poets of the Welsh Princes* (Cardiff, 1978).

Williams, Glanmor, *The Welsh Church from Conquest to Reformation* (2nd edn, Cardiff, 1976).

Williams, G., *Welsh Poetry, Sixth Century to 1600* (1973).

Wright, T. (ed.), *A Selection of Latin Stories* (Percy Society, 8, 1842).

Wynn, John, Sir, *The History of the Gwydir Family, and Memoirs*, ed. Jones, J.G. (Llandysul, 1990).

Index

A

Aber, court of 106
Aberffraw, court of 26, 27, 105, 106
   church of 132
Aberlleiniog, castle of 16
Abermenai 55
Aberystwyth, castle of 34, 55, 102
Abingdon, abbey of 116
Adeliza, widow of Richard fitzGilbert 43, 61
Aeron, river 42
Alexander III, Pope 85, 111, 118, 119
Anarawd ap Gruffudd ap Rhys 41, 47, 54, 115
   daughter of 55
Anglesey (Môn) 15, 16, 18, 26, 55, 60, 69, 105, 106, 107, 128
   men of 71
   nobles of 14
Anglo-Norman Marcher Lords 67–68, 75, 78, 81, 82, 83, 105
Anglo-Saxon kingship 12
Anglo-Saxon, chronicle 12
Anjou 61, 64, 66, 79, 88
Aquitaine 93
Ardudwy 17, 18
Arfon 26, 106, 107
Arllechwedd 18
Arnulf, bishop of Lisieux 93
Arthur of Bardsey 117–118

Arwystli 11, 14, 15, 30, 62, 73
Asser 107
Avranches, Hugh of, earl of Chester 15, 16, 18

B

Baldwin, archbishop of Canterbury 127
Bangor 106, 114, 117, 132
   archdeacon of 114, 118, 119
   bishop of 113, 114
   cathedral 33, 126–127, 132
Bardsey 117, 118, 132
Basingwerk 68, 69
   abbey of 132
   castle of 72, 82
Beaumont, Robert de 72
Bec, Walter de 34
Becket, Thomas, archbishop of Canterbury 29, 78, 85, 87–88, 101, 111, 112, 116, 117–120, 123, 127, 133
Bernard, bishop of St David's 111, 115, 116–117
Berwyn mountains 79, 90
Bleddyn ap Cynfyn 14
Brecon 17, 43
   castle of 43
Bretons 93
Bron-yr-Erw, battle of 15
Brycheiniog 11, 38, 39

Index

C

Cadell ap Gruffudd ap Rhys 41
Cadfan ap Cadwaladr 58, 60
Cadwallon ap Gruffudd ap Cynan 20, 22, 24, 25, 30, 32-33, 35
Cadwallon ap Madog 73
Cadwallon ab Owain Gwynedd 80
Cadwaladr ap Gruffudd ap Cynan 22, 24, 30, 31-32, 33, 34-36, 38-48, 51*ff.*, 69, 71-73, 81, 98, 102, 103, 107, 112, 115, 117, 127, 128, 132
Cadwgan ap Gronw ab Owain 30
Cadwgan ap Goronwy 33, 99
Caereinion, lordship of 82
Caer Gybi 132
Caerwedros, castle of 34
Canterbury, Gervase of 70, 79
Cantref Mawr 77
Caradog ap Gruffudd ap Rhydderch 11, 12, 13, 14, 15, 38
Cardigan 48
  castle of 39, 40, 41, 42, 43, 44, 47, 55
  town of 40
  Stephen, constable of 39
Carmarthen 40, 44
Ceiriog Valley 79
Ceredigion 17, 26, 39, 43, 44, 54, 55, 58, 61, 68, 78, 103, 106
  campaigns in 34-36, 38-39, 98, 102-103
  Norman castles in 40
Champfleury, Hugh de 89-90, 111, 113
Chester 14, 16, 48, 68, 83, 116
  Benedictine house in 132
  castle of 70
  earls of 15, 18, 19, 20, 44, 58, 132

Ranulf, earl of 44, 46, 47, 48, 49, 60, 61
Chichester, bishop of 115
Church 28, 29
  patronage of 28
Clare, family of 36
  Baldwin fitzGilbert 43, 47
  Gilbert fitzRichard 36, 37
  Richard fitzGilbert 37-38, 40, 42, 43, 47, 61
Clynnog Fawr 15, 114, 132
Coed Grono 38
Coggeshall, Ralph of 81
Coleshill, battle of 49, 60, 70
Conwy, river 15, 16, 18
Cornwall, earl of 73
Corwen 79
Courcy, Robert de 70
Cronica Walliae 60
Cunedda ap Cadwallon 59, 63
Crug Mawr, battle at 39
Cydweli, battle at 39
Cyfeiliog, lordship of 73-74, 99
Cynan, son of Iago 13-14
Cynan ab Owain Gwynedd 48, 57, 58-59, 70, 73, 102, 128
Cynddelw Brydydd Mawr 129, 133
Cynfael, castle of 57, 104
Cynwrig ap Rhiwallon 14, 15

D

Dafydd ab Owain Gwynedd 70, 78, 102, 128
Daniel ap Llosgwrn 129
David, bishop of Bangor 114
David, archdeacon of Bangor 119
Dee, river 15, 48, 83
Deheubarth 11, 15, 21, 22, 36, 39,

47, 48, 49, 61, 62, 65, 67, 68, 72, 73, 79, 94, 96, 115
Denmark 21, 101
Diceto, Ralph of 74, 77, 94
Dineirth, castle of 34
Dinllaen, commote of 54
Dublin 13, 55, 56, 80
Dyfed 17
Dyffryn Clwyd 17, 19, 22, 35, 49, 68
Dyfi, river 36, 38, 40, 42

E

Eifionydd 17, 18
Einion Clud 73
Einion ab Owain 33
Elfael 38, 39
Essex, Henry of 70
Ewyas 43

F

fitzHarold, Richard 43
fitzJohn, Eustace 70
fitzJohn, Payn 44
Flanders 79
Flemings 36, 40, 93
French 11, 12, 16, 18, 21, 36, 50, 71, 78, 93

G

Gascony 79, 93
Geddington 75
Gesta Stephani 40, 43, 46
Gilbert, bishop of St Asaph 116
Gloucester 75
    Robert, earl of 43
    Miles of 43
Godfrey, bishop of St Asaph 116

Godwinson, Harold, earl of Wessex and king of England 12
Gogynfeirdd 29
Gronw ab Owain 30, 118
Goronwy ab Owain ab Edwin 19, 20
Gruffudd ap Cynan 13–23, 26, 27, 29, 30, 31, 34, 44, 53, 96, 98, 99, 100–101, 104, 106, 107, 122, 123, 128, 132
    Angharad, wife of 17, 24, 55, 56, 129, 130, 131
    court of 21, 29
    daughter of, Gwenllian 39
    death of 33, 41, 54
    sons of 39, 51
    Statute of 28
    teulu of 17
Gruffudd ap Llywelyn 12, 13, 14, 99
Gruffudd ap Rhys ap Tewdwr 21, 39, 40, 41, 54
    sons of 47
Gwaederw, battle of 15
Gwalchmai ap Meilyr 122, 130
Gwgon 107
Gwion, bishop of Bangor 127
Gwynedd 11, 13, 14, 15, 17, 23, 30, 35, 39, 42, 60, 62, 67, 68, 79, 86, 94, 96, 97, 101, 104, 107, 111, 114, 127
    castles in 104
    civil war in 47
    clergy in 118
    Is Conwy 19, 68, 106
    Uwch Conwy 18, 19, 68, 106
    troops from 40, 41, 49
Gwynllŵg 11, 12, 38, 46

Index

H
Hastings, battle of (1066) 11, 12
Haughmond, abbey of 61, 112, 132
Hawarden 70
Henry I, king of England 18, 19–21, 29, 34 36–37, 42, 43, 44, 62, 73, 101
Henry II, king of England 29, 49–50, 61, 62, 64*ff.*, 85*ff.*, 97, 107, 111, 112, 123, 125
Henri ab Arthen 28
Hereford 14
    bishop of 115
Hexham, John of 43, 44, 46
Hiberno-Scandinavians 13, 15, 41, 55, 56, 80, 87, 92
    chiefs of, Otir, Turcaill and Cherwulf 55
Historia vab Kenan 13, 18, 22, 23, 29, 32, 33, 99, 100–101, 104, 106, 107
Historia gloriosi Regis Ludovici VII 78
Hywel Dda 108
Hywel ap Maredudd 38
Hywel ab Ieuaf 62, 73
Hywel ab Owain Gwynedd 26, 29, 31, 42, 48, 55, 57–58, 59–60, 73, 102, 103, 127, 128
Hywel ap Rhys ap Tewdwr 21

I
Iago ab Idwal ap Meurig 13
Iâl, lordship of 49, 72, 106
Iorwerth Goch 72
Ireland 13, 15, 17, 21, 55, 60, 80, 101, 104, 117, 118
Irish Sea 92

J
John I, king of England 97

L
Leicester, earl of 72
Lincoln, city of 46
    battle of 46, 48, 61
Lincolnshire 45
    Welsh troops in 45
Lisieux, bishop of 93
Loughor 43
Llanbadarn Fawr 28, 36
Llandaff 114
Llaneilian 132
Llanrhystud, castle of 58, 104
Llyfr Cyfnerth 31
Llwyd, Humphrey 60
Llŷn 16, 17, 18, 26, 54, 106, 107
    nobles of 14, 15
Llywarch ap Trahaearn 30
Llywelyn the Great 25, 128
Llywelyn the Last 25
Louis VII, king of France 29, 84*ff.*, 97, 101, 111, 113, 120, 125
Lucy, Richard de 72

M
Madog ab Idnerth 38
Madog ap Maredudd 46, 49, 62, 72, 74
Malcolm, king of Scotland 74
Matilda, daughter of Henry I 42, 44, 45–46, 61, 67
Maelienydd 38, 39, 73
Magnus Bareleg, king of Norway 17
Maredudd ap Bleddyn 21
Maredudd ap Gruffudd 96

Maredudd ap Hywel ap Maredudd 38
Maredudd ab Owain 11
Mawddach, river 58
Meirion 107
Meirion Goch 16
Meirionydd 22, 32, 36, 54, 57, 58, 59, 62, 68, 99, 106, 128
Merwydd, sons of 107
Meurig, bishop of Bangor 113, 115–116, 117
Meylir Brydydd, court poet 27
Meylir ab Owain ab Edwin 19
Meylir ap Rhiwallon 15
Moelfre 70
Mold, castle of 48
Montgomery, Hugh de, earl of Shrewsbury 17
    Roger de, earl of Shrewsbury 18
Montmirail 95
Morfran 57
Morgan ab Owain 38, 46
Morgannwg 11
Murchadh, king of Ireland 21, 101
Mynydd Carn, battle of 15

N

Nanheudwy 33
Neath, river 40
Nefyn, castle of 16
Newburgh, William of 80
Normans 11, 12, 13, 14, 38, 39, 62, 66, 69, 70, 73, 93
Northampton 48

O

Ostia, bishop of 78
Owain ab Edwin 16, 17, 19, 24
Owain Cyfeiliog 82, 96, 124
Owain Gwynedd (ap Gruffudd ap Cynan) 22, 24
birth 25–26
    Cadwaladr 51–63
Ceredigion, campaigns in 34–36, 38, 39–41
church 112–120
court of 104–106
death of 95, 120, 121, 126–127
early life 26–32
government and administration of 108–110
Guiradus, servant of 90, 113
Henry II 64–83
kingship 51–54
laws of 108–109
Louis VII 84–95
Montmirail 95
Morfran 57
Moses, servant of 89, 113
opinions of 24
reputation 121–34
rule of 96ff., 108–109
title[s] of 111–113
wives of, Gwladus and Cristin 30, 118, 130
Owain Glyndŵr 25
Oxford 75

P

Paris 28, 113
Pembrokeshire 15, 40
Penmon 132
Pentraeth, battle of 128
Poitevins 93

Index

Powys 11, 21, 22, 33, 46, 49, 58, 62, 67, 72, 74, 79, 82, 96
Prestatyn, castle of 72, 82

R

Ragnhildr 13
Reginald, earl of Cornwall 73
Rhiwallon ap Cynfyn 14
Rhodri Mawr 128
Rhos 17, 22, 35
Rhuddlan 70
Robert of 14–15, 16, 19
   castle and *llys* of 15, 72, 82
Rhufoniog 19, 22, 35
Rhun ab Owain Gwynedd 59, 129, 130
Rhwng Gwy a Hafren 11
Rhygyfarch the Wise 28
Rhymni, river 11
Rhiryd ab Owain ab Edwin 19
Rhys ap Gruffudd (Lord Rhys) 65, 69, 73, 74, 77, 82, 89, 94, 95, 124
Rhys ap Hywel ap Maredudd 38
Rhys ab Owain Gwynedd 80
Rhys ap Tewdwr 15, 17, 36
Richard I, king of England 97
Richard de la Mare 34
Richard, son of Hugh, earl of Chester 20

S

St Asaph 70, 114, 116, 117
St David's 28, 114, 115, 117
Salisbury, John of 94
Scots 93
Seisyll Bryffwrch 129
Severn, river 92

Shrewsbury 14, 61, 112
   Benedictine house in 132
   earl of 17, 18
Shropshire 61
   Ness in 61–62
   Sheriff of 44
Sihtricson, Olaf, king of Dublin 13
Simon of Clynnog 114, 115
Soissons, bishop of 89, 111
Stephen, king of England (of Blois) 42–43, 44, 45, 46, 47, 48, 49, 60, 61, 64, 66, 67, 115
Sulien, bishop 28
Sussex 44

T

Tafolwern, castle of 73
Tegeingl 17, 19, 30, 44, 48, 49, 71, 72, 78, 82–83, 106
Teifi, river 37, 58
Theobald, archbishop of Canterbury 115, 116, 118
Tomen y Rhodwydd, castle of 49, 72, 104
Tonbridge 36
Toringy, Robert de 71, 77, 89
Trahaearn ap Caradog 14, 15
Tywi, valley of 41
Tywyn 104
   clas church of 57, 132

U

Uchtryd ab Edwin 16, 99

V

Vitalis, Orderic, Anglo-Norman chronicler 13, 16, 20, 45, 46–47, 51, 53

157

W

Wales, invasion of 16
Wales, Gerald of (Gerald de Barri)
    31, 37–38, 40, 71, 74, 92, 97, 105,
    123–124, 126–127
Wallingford, Brian de 38
Welsh chroniclers 11, 16, 21, 34, 53,
    56, 59, 60, 65, 101
William I, duke of Normandy and
    king of England 12, 14
William II, king of England 16, 37
Woodstock 74–75, 77, 85, 88, 94
Worcester, castle of 73
    cathedral of 115

Y

Ystrad Alun 44, 48, 49, 68
Ystrad Tywi 17, 39
Ystwyth, river 37

Owain Gwynedd is just one of a whole range of publications from Y Lolfa. For a full list of books currently in print, send now for your free copy of our new full-colour catalogue. Or simply surf into our website

www.ylolfa.com

for secure on-line searching and ordering.

ylolfa

TALYBONT CEREDIGION CYMRU SY24 5HE
e-mail ylolfa@ylolfa.com
website www.ylolfa.com
phone (01970) 832 304
fax 832 782